getting laid

getting laid

Everything You Need to Know

about Raising Chickens, Gardening

and Preserving

—With Over 100 Recipes

By Barb Webb

viva

EDITIONS

Published in the United States by Viva Editions, an imprint of Start Midnight, LLC, 375 Hudson Street, Twelfth Floor, New York, New York 10014.

Printed in the United States.
Cover design: Scott Idleman/Blink
Cover photograph: Life on White/Getty Images & iStockphoto
Text design: Frank Wiedemann
First Edition.
10 9 8 7 6 5 4 3 2 1

Trade paper ISBN: 978-1-63228-021-3
E-book ISBN: 978-1-63228-028-2

Library of Congress Cataloging-in-Publication Data is available.

The recipes contained in this book have been created for the ingredients and techniques indicated. The Publisher is not responsible for your specific health or allergy needs that may require medical supervision. You are, of course, free to make substitutions or modifications to suit your personal dietary needs or tastes. However, the Publisher shall not be responsible for any adverse reactions that you may suffer, whether to the recipes as contained in this book or as modified by you.

To the chickens that have graced our homestead, I'm indebted to your wise teachings. To the powers above and the earth below, I am grateful for your abundant blessings. To my husband, my children, and all the amazing people in my life, I am thankful for your support and your love, which sustain me.

Contents

1. Get Started: Living a Sexy Sustainable Lifestyle. 1

2. Get Laid: Raising Your Chicken Brood 9

3. Get Fowl: Caring for Your Chickens. 33

4. Get Dirty: Growing Your Garden of Eden 49

5. Get Cured: Preserving Your Bounty. 89

6. Get Fried: Dishing Up Poultry and Eggs in the Kitchen 141

7. Get Fed: Preparing Your Garden Harvest 175

8. Get Baked: Creating Artisan Breads and Sweets. 199

9. Get Wild: Celebrating Your DIY Style. 225

10. Get Real: Assessing Your Sexy Sustainable Lifestyle. 261

Recipe and Instruction Index 265

About the Author 269

1. Get Started:
Living a Sexy
Sustainable Lifestyle

The world is mud-luscious and puddle-wonderful.
—e.e. cummings

There are four simple facts that govern this guide:

1. Baby chicks are crazy-huggable-adorable and they grow up to be beautiful, bountiful chickens.

2. Everything fresh and organic looks, tastes, and *is* better for you.

3. Conserving our natural resources is vital to the future of our planet and better for our pocketbooks.

4. Sexy doesn't come from a bottle or a well-fitted brassiere. It radiates from inside and illuminates the world through our actions and choices.

Sustainable living has acquired a bit of a bad rap over the years. From extremist position visions of zombie apocalypse shelters to real little houses on the prairie—any way you slice it, the vision often doesn't mesh well with the advances of our modern world.

As someone who grew up watching *Little House on the Prairie*, I certainly daydreamed about hanging out in that simpler time, but it wasn't as if I was willing to give up my Billy Idol T-shirt or *Star Wars* figure collection to get there.

Though I opt to embrace a sustainable lifestyle today, I'm still resistant to giving up certain things like my smartphone or dishwasher. Instead, I make informed decisions about the products I purchase; reduce energy use whenever and wherever possible; and reuse, repurpose, and recycle. To conserve resources, grow your own food, raise your own backyard chickens, and utilize all the glorious tools nature gives us is not only practical, it's doable!

Sustainable living boasts no boundaries. You don't need massive amounts of acreage or even a fenced-in backyard. We may not be 100 percent sustainable in our lifestyles, but we can become better in tune with our environment and conscientious about our actions. Like all aspects of life, it's about balance, finding ways to live a greener, cleaner life within the parameters of our current lifestyles.

There's no need to turn your world topsy-turvy or morph into Laura Ingalls Wilder overnight. Simply make one decision right now—and you've already accomplished that by picking up this guide. Bravo!

Make another change tomorrow, then another, and so on…. Each step will lead you toward reducing your eco-footprint. Each step will lead you toward a lighter, greener, sexier you—a modern, sustainable chick who embraces change and flaunts her eco-savvy chic!

WHY DO YOU WANT TO LIVE A SUSTAINABLE LIFESTYLE?

What initially drew you to the idea of raising chickens, organic gardening and incorporating more sustainable-living practices into your lifestyle? Are you interested in saving money, eating a more healthy diet, being on trend, going more "green," or saving the planet one plant at a time?

Whatever the reason, the good news is that all of the above motivators are real, tangible end-results of sustainable living.

What does sustainable living mean? When you think about the term, what definition would you choose? (Circle the definition you feel fits best.)

Sustainable living is...

a) reducing your carbon footprint
b) eating organic and "living off the land"
c) living in harmony with the earth
d) using resources efficiently and investing in renewable resources
e) creating a better future for the next generation
f) protecting and nurturing our natural resources
g) eliminating waste and recycling
h) actively pursuing a simple and balanced lifestyle
i) spending money and resources in a frugal way
j) our economy, social structure, and natural environment working in agreement for the betterment of the world

If you circled all of the above answers, you are correct! Sustainable living has many definitions and interpretations that have developed over time. The Merriam Webster Dictionary defines sustainable as "able to be used without being completely used up or destroyed" and living as "full of life or vigor."

In a nutshell, as sustainable-living agents, we are ultimately defenders, maintainers, and supporters of life!

Our mission is of the utmost importance to ourselves, our environment, and our future generations. Our mission is also easy. In fact, it takes less than five minutes to incorporate one sustainable-living practice into your life right now, but the effect of your action may have an everlasting positive impact for the world.

PUSH DOWN ON THE SAFETY BAR AND HOLD ON TIGHT! WE ARE ON THIS SUSTAINABLE RIDE TOGETHER

Let me tell you a secret. It's honestly amusing to me that my life has brought me to this crazy-cool juncture where I find myself writing a book on sustainable living and chickens.

Twenty years ago, the closest I got to a farm or a chicken was when I picked up a fresh package of meat from the butcher. I was a big-city gal, with minuscule exposure to raising animals. The landscape changed dramatically when I relocated to a rural area and saw the first little coop full of fluffy chicks. It was truly love at first peep!

The nurturing I did have, though, came from the three women who influenced my love of nature and do-it-yourself—my maternal and paternal grandmothers and my mother. These vivacious, creative women used the resources available to them in amazingly clever ways. Though we were pocketbook-poor, I had a rich childhood full of hearty meals, handmade clothes, and artisan crafts. Long before sustainable living became a popular trend, these dynamic women, along with others from their generations, defined frugal living and eco-friendly habits.

My father, who was a hunter, a fisherman, and an avid baker, opened up my initial propensity toward exploring new foods and opened my eyes to how food actually landed on our dinner plates. More than that, though, he drilled within me the understanding of personal responsibility to ourselves, to others, and to our environment.

Admittedly, I resisted these lessons in my formative years. They took decades to sink in, but nonetheless I am grateful for these incredible individuals who lovingly guided me toward the person I am—the person you are embarking on this journey with today.

Every iota of information, every word, every recipe, every thought in this book I owe to those who guided me, who shared their thoughts and ideas, and who encouraged me to explore the world around me. I owe plenty of thanks to the earth that continues to supply a wonderful bounty in our garden and the chickens in our coop who have nourished our family and taught me so much about their way of life. There's a lot to be said about meandering around the yard, eating only what you find in your immediate environment, and roosting on a regular schedule each night. Imagine if we embraced their teachings and mastered the art of chicken Zen!

Initially, I wanted to begin this guide by telling you all the cool and clever things you'll find contained within the pages, but that's kind of mean. It's like showing you the end of the movie in the preview clip, then making you watch the whole film just to realize you already saw all the good stuff happen.

Not what I envisioned. Certainly not what you deserve.

What I envision for us is a journey. One where you discover the secrets. One where you write the script. One where you determine what happens next and how the story ends.

There's nothing tricky, gimmicky, or complex about this guide, and that's part of what's so sexy! There are no limits to how far you can take things. What you will find are fun, manageable, and inspiring ideas you can easily incorporate into your current lifestyle.

Materials presented in this book may be a little outside the norm, but that's all part of the allure! For our modern world, sustainable living deserves a modern approach and a realistic attitude. The truth is, you can integrate a sustainable lifestyle into your current lifestyle, without self-deprivation or turning your back on all the wonderful advancements in our industrialized world. In fact, many of these advancements, such as home hydroponics and apartment-friendly compost bins, allow us to easily implement eco-friendly practices in our homes.

You may not be able to power your home with a windmill, commute twenty miles to work on a bicycle made from recycled landfill parts, or give up your love of the latest fashions, but that doesn't mean sustainable living isn't for you. You can still ride that bike on the weekends to the farmers market, detoxify the air in your home with the right container garden, and urge your favorite clothing company to adopt environmentally friendly practices.

Ultimately, we *are* responsible for our personal choices. We can alter our lifestyles to incorporate more natural, beautiful practices. Collectively, we can evaluate the impact of our choices and modify our environment for the greater good of ourselves, our communities, and the entire world.

The key is to start—and you already have! Right now you are laying the foundation for your personal, contemporary Garden of Eden.

Begin reading at any section of any chapter, or choose conventional wisdom and absorb each page in this book from beginning to end. It's your journey. Now, let's get started on the path to a more sustainable, sexy you!

TEN WAYS TO LIVE A MORE SUSTAINABLE LIFESTYLE IN THE NEXT FIVE MINUTES

Pick one activity and simply make the effort to do it. Five minutes from now, you'll be a sexier sustainable chick. Seriously, five minutes, that's it. Now get to it!

1. Permanently say *hasta la vista* to paper and plastic bags. Slip a reusable bag into your purse, briefcase, or backpack and keep several in your car. Most importantly—use them! (Don't have any? Flip to Chapter 9, Get Wild, for instructions on how to turn a T-shirt into a reusable bag.)

If you eliminate three plastic shopping bags per week by using reusable bags, that's more than 150 plastic bags per year that you will rescue from the landfill. Considering that it takes around 1,000 years for a plastic bag to decompose, that's one high-impact rescue!

2. Put your mailbox on a diet. Register to opt out of receiving unsolicited mail. Visit optoutprescreen.com to choose a five-year or permanent solution. Pay your bills online and enroll in paper-free statements from your bank and credit card companies.

Junk mail production requires vast amounts of timber and water. For each piece you eliminate, you are protecting earth's valuable resources. And, really, how many credit card offers does one person need?

3. Chill out with your laundry. Wash clothes during the nonpeak hours of 6–8 a.m. and 8–10 p.m., when possible. Use only cold water to wash clothing. Take it one step further and use a clothesline or drying rack to dry your clothes.

According to Energy Star, about 90 percent of the energy consumed by a washing machine goes to heating water. Each time you make the switch from warm to cold water, you are eliminating carbon dioxide emissions and conserving our precious resources.

4. Go ninja on your appliances. Not like crazy hand-to-hand combat ninja, but stealth ninja by unplugging all appliances when they are not in use. Make it easy by using power strips for multiple items like coffee makers, toasters, printers, and computers; then just unplug the power strip when you are finished using the appliances.

Many appliances consume only a watt or two when left plugged in, but the cumulative effect of all your appliances has a big impact—as much as 5 to 10 percent of your electric bill. Assuming that the average electric bill is $150 per month, that represents a savings of $90 to $180 a year. Unplugging is not only great for the environment; it's highly beneficial to your budget bottom line!

5. Enjoy your fruits and veggies "au naturel." Choose to grow and purchase organic. As the demand for organic produce increases, companies that support organic methods thrive, and the environmental effect is a positive one. For starters, studies show that, if ten thousand small and medium-size farms convert to sustainable organic practices, the environmental effect in terms of carbon sequestration is the equivalent of removing more than one million cars from the road.

Flip to Chapter 4 (Get Dirty) to start your organic garden today!

6. Keep the home fires burning—responsibly. Turn the temperature in your residence down (heat) or up (cool) a few degrees. Adjust the temperature down a few degrees on your water heater. You'll never notice the difference, but your electric bill will!

7. Put your culinary wizard hat on. Make a meal from scratch to replace one prepackaged meal. You'll find plenty of recipe inspirations in Chapter 7 (Get Fed) and Chapter 8 (Get Baked).

Cooking at home offers you full control over the ingredients and is less expensive than eating out or purchasing prepackaged foods. Homemade meals are also better for the environment, as you expend less energy and resources.

8. Go dancing in the dark. Convert your light bulbs to LED's or CFL's for more energy-efficient lighting. Better yet, turn off the lights. Open up the shades and let natural lighting in. If it is nighttime and you need just a little bit of light, use a natural (toxin-free) candle to create a romantic and stress-reducing glow.

9. Make a beautiful day in your neighborhood. Need produce or products? Buy local goods today. Visit your farmers market or stores offering local goods.

Producing, processing, and packaging foods and goods expends energy, but transporting it adds a huge amount of fuel consumption to the bill. When we purchase local items, it minimizes the transportation costs and helps our community thrive.

10. Turn the page and continue your sustainable-living journey! Every chicken you raise, seed you grow, food you preserve, easy recipe you make, scrap you compost, product you upcycle, or gift you make yourself enhances your life with rich, natural benefits and healthy rewards for your body and the environment.

2. Get Laid:

Raising Your Chicken Brood

Rich hues, jewel tones, lace patterns, Mediterranean and Asiatic origins—evocative words that could easily describe runway fashions or upcoming designer trends. Surprisingly, they're also terms used to describe characteristics of chickens.

If you've had any hesitations as to whether raising chicks would cramp your style, jettison them. Nothing makes a bold fashion statement like a vibrant chicken ruffling its feathers and pecking at bugs in your yard. They are totally the hot new lawn ornaments of the twenty-first century sustainable home!

WHAT'S YOUR CHICKEN STYLE?

As every fashionista knows, you first have to determine what you are shopping for before you can zero in on a style that flatters you. In chicken-speak, this means you need to first decide what aspect of raising chickens appeals to you the most. Will you be raising chickens for eggs, meat, show, breeding, rescue, or a combination of several of these elements?

Take this mini-quiz to begin your path to selecting the best chicken match for your style.

Circle the number of the answer that you best identify with:

How would you classify your fashion sensibilities?
1. Trendy
2. Classic

3. Functional
4. Glamorous
5. Casual
6. Natural

What fashion item appeals to you most?
1. Neon-blue tights
2. Sweater set
3. Reversible rain jacket
4. Jewel-encrusted cuff bracelet
5. Faded denim jeans
6. Hemp woven T-shirt

How often do you prefer to update your wardrobe?
1. Seasonally
2. Once per year
3. Every three to five years
4. Whenever you can afford the luxury item you have your eye on
5. When you are not too busy with the needs of others
6. Only when it is in need of dire repair

You invite your friends over for a party; what do you like to serve?
1. Barbecue fresh from the grill
2. Quiche with fresh herbs
3. Brunch—a little something for everyone
4. Port wine and Brie
5. Homemade beef stew with dumplings, and peach cobbler for dessert
6. A spinach soufflé with mushrooms you foraged in the morning

Scoring: Give yourself one point for each 1–6 answer. Tally up the points for each. The number with the most points is your style match.

1 _____ 2 _____ 3 _____ 4 _____ 5 _____ 6 _____

Mostly 1's: Rapidly changing fashion is your passion. With each new season comes a new reason to start fresh. Raising chickens for meat is your perfect trendy match. Meat chickens typically require a short two-to-four-month commitment before moving on to selecting and raising the next brood.

Mostly 2's: A timeless classic, you gravitate toward styles you can make use of season after season. If you are in it for the long haul (three to four years), raising chickens for eggs is going to be your forte.

Mostly 3's: Flexible fashions capture your interest. You love dual-purpose things, like scarves that can do double duty as belts and backpacks that open up to become picnic blankets. Combo meat-egg chickens will be your best coop accessory. You'll get a little bit of the best of both with a shorter time commitment (six months to two years), rather than raising eggs-only chickens.

Mostly 4's: The spotlight is on you! You're a glamour girl who loves showing off your exotic finds from far-flung shopping trips. Show chickens are right up your glitter-filled alley.

Mostly 5's: A nurturer at heart, you're the first to volunteer your time and are not afraid to get a little dirt on your comfortable shoes in the process. Raising chicks for breeding could be your dream job. You might be reluctant to let the little ones fly the coop when they are ready, but on the flip side—you'll never have empty-nest syndrome.

Mostly 6's: Rescuing garments from the local thrift shop rocks your fashion world. Raising endangered chickens might be the type of exciting challenge you live for. The commitment can be intense, but the rewards are truly remarkable.

WHAT IF MY NUMBERS DON'T MATCH UP?

If you wound up with a split number preference, such as two tallies in the number 2 and 4 slots, you can certainly join your interests and look for show chickens that have high egg production.

If you don't feel your answer suits you—for example, you selected all 1's, but you really don't think you want to raise meat chickens and would rather have egg layers—no worries! This quiz is designed to offer a general informational overview and an idea of how your chicken-raising interests might match up with your personal style preferences.

The key part of this exercise is to guide you toward making a choice. Prior to raising chickens and selecting a breed to purchase, it's important to have a clear idea of why you will be raising your chickens. To wind up with a profuse egg-laying breed when what you really wanted was chickens for meat will create a less than ideal relationship for you and your new feathered friends.

Now that you know whether you are aiming to raise chickens for eggs, meat, breeding, show, or rescue, it's time to delve a little deeper into additional areas that will affect your purchase decisions.

DOES THAT BREED MATCH MY HANDBAG?

Just like a new line of your favorite designer's fall fashions, when you first see a box full of adorable baby chicks, it's tempting to simply gather them up and bring them all home. If you don't know what those babies will grow into, though, you could easily find yourself in full panic with a yard full of mismatched broody hens and feisty roosters.

The handy charts at the end of this section will help you quickly identify breeds, types, egg and feather colors, and origin, to help you make a sound selection. All these factors can affect your chicken style decisions.

TOP TEN DO'S AND DON'T'S FOR CHICKEN DIVAS

Don't overdo it. Start with a small brood of chickens (six to twelve). This will give you time to enjoy your introduction phase and decide if raising chickens is really for you, without being overwhelmed.

Do search the internet or consult the American Standard of Perfection published by the American Poultry Association for pictures and full descriptions of recognized chicken breeds and varieties. You'll gain a full understanding of what your chicks will morph into as they mature. Check your local library, 4H, or farm agency for access to a copy.

Do stick to a single breed if you plan to have a breeding flock. You'll get the best results. Cross-breeding can cause numerous problems and inconsistent outcomes.

Don't be afraid to mix chickens if you are not breeding. If raised together, hens will cohabitate in peace.

Do look for different ways to incorporate chickens into your lifestyle. Even if you have a small backyard or only a rooftop patio, there's still a coop for you!

Don't get a rooster unless you need one to protect your flock from predators or to fertilize the eggs for breeding. Hens will produce eggs without the aid of a rooster.

Don't purchase multiple roosters unless you are breeding for meat. Roosters are territorial and, upon maturity, will begin fighting with each other. They also have a tendency to become aggressive toward owners and literally bite the hand that feeds them!

Do take a chance on endangered breeds. They may take a little more effort to raise but the rewards of contributing to a breed's survival are rich.

Don't underestimate how attractive a yard full of colorful chickens can be. They will not only beautify your yard and provide you with sustenance, but they'll keep your bug population down too.

Do look for breeds with feather accents like lace or barring (stripes) to amp up the luxe factor of your chicken fashion!

If you are a true chicken fashion diva, there's one more rule to keep in mind: *Don't* try an all dark-feathered yard full of chickens unless you're into that whole biker-babe or goth trend. Eco-girlfriend, there's simply no such thing as a basic little black chicken coop dress!

 Chick Tip: Sooner or later, you'll begin to notice chicken feathers lying around your coop, particularly during molting season, when you will discover mounds of them. Instead of composting them or letting the wind carry them off, pick the feathers up, dust them off and try repurposing them in one of these clever ways:

1. Construct a decorative feather fan
2. Embellish your card crafts
3. Make a Mardi Gras masquerade mask
4. String together a feather boa
5. Create textured writing paper
6. Design a unique wall hanging
7. Stuff a throw pillow
8. Decorate a hat brim
9. Tuck them into flower arrangements
10. Decorate your scrapbook pages
11. Use as material for fashioning hair accessories
12. Fabricate a feather wreath

CHICKEN STYLE GUIDES

Readers scoring mostly 1's, 2's or 3's on the chicken style mini-quiz (p. 9), this list is for you:

Quick Guide to Common Egg and Meat Chickens				
BREED	**TYPE**	**EGG COLOR**	**ORIGIN**	**FEATHER COLOR**
Ancona	Egg	White	Italy	Black/White
Araucana	Egg	Multi	South America	Black/Red
Australorp	Duo	Light Brown	Australia	Black/Blue
Barnvelder	Egg	Reddish Brown	Holland	Multi
Brahma	Duo	Light Brown	China	Buff
Cochin	Duo	Light Brown	Asia	Black/Multi
Cornish	Meat	Pale Cream	United Kingdom	Multi
Cream Legbar	Egg	Blue, Green	United Kingdom	Crele
Croad Langshan	Duo	Plum	China	Blue, Black, White
Dominique	Duo	Brown	USA	Black/White
Dorking	Duo	White	United Kingdom	Multi
Faverolles	Duo	Light Brown	France	Salmon
Hamburg	Egg	White	Europe	Gold/Silver
Jersey Giant	Duo	Brown	USA	Black/Blue

Leghorn	Egg	White	Italy	Multi
Marans	Egg	Dark Brown	France	Black/Multi
Minorca	Egg	White	Mediterranean	Black/White
New Hampshire	Duo	Light Brown	USA	Reddish Brown
Orpington	Meat	Pinkish Brown	United Kingdom	Buff/Multi
Plymouth Rock	Duo	Tinted	USA	Black/White
Rhode Island Red	Duo	Medium Brown	USA	Red
Rhode Island White	Duo	Medium Brown	USA	White
Silkie	Egg	Pale Cream	Asia	Multi
Sussex	Duo	Light Brown	United Kingdom	Brown/ Multi
Welsummer	Duo	Dark Brown	Holland	Partridge
Wyandotte	Duo	Light Brown	USA	Black/ White/Multi

 Chick Tip: Chickens listed as "egg" or "meat" types excel at their indicated purpose. Meat types may lay eggs, but they are most often infrequent layers or the eggs are small in size. Egg layers may be used for meat but will generally be slower growers, and by the time they are ready for meat processing, the meat may be tough. A general misconception of new chicken owners is that layers will be ideal meat chickens when they reach the end of their egg laying days. These chickens are still edible and may be butchered, but will be suitable mainly for stewing.

Chickens listed as "duo" offer a good mix of both egg and meat qualities. They may produce fewer eggs or take longer to mature for meat processing, but are still highly suitable for both.

Readers scoring mostly 4's on the chicken style mini-quiz (p. 9), this list is for you:

Quick Guide to Popular Show Chickens				
BREED	**TYPE**	**EGG COLOR**	**ORIGIN**	**FEATHER COLOR**
Brahma	Duo	Light Brown	China	Buff
Cochin	Duo	Light Brown	Asia	Black/Multi
Croad Langshan	Duo	Plum	China	Blue, Black, White
Cubalaya	Egg	White	Cuba	Black, Blue/Red
Dominique	Duo	Brown	USA	Black/White
Dutch Bantam	Ornamental	Light Brown	Netherlands	Silver, Yellow, Red
Favorelles	Duo	Light Brown	France	Salmon
Java	Duo	Brown	USA	Auburn, Black, White
Malay	Game	Tinted	Asia	White, Red, Black
Orpington	Meat	Pinkish Brown	United Kingdom	Buff/Multi
Silver Phoenix	Ornamental	Cream	Japan	Multi

Chick Tip: As you will note, many show chickens are appropriate for other types of chicken raising in addition to being ornamental (show) pets. If you decide that having a show chicken is not desirable, you'll have the flexibility to change course and raise the chicks as egg or meat chickens instead. In the case of "egg" or "duo" types, you'll simply get to enjoy the best of show and regular fresh eggs too!

Readers scoring mostly 5's on the chicken style mini-quiz (p. 9), this list is for you:

Quick Guide to the Most Motherly Hens				
BREED	**TYPE**	**EGG COLOR**	**ORIGIN**	**FEATHER COLOR**
Araucana	Egg	Multi	South America	Black/Red
Assel	Game	Pale Cream	India	Dark Red, Multi
Australorpe	Duo	Light Brown	Australia	Black/Blue
Cochin	Duo	Light Brown	Asia	Black/Multi
Cream Legbar	Egg	Blue, Green	United Kingdom	Crele
Croad Langshan	Duo	Plum	China	Blue, Black, White
Delaware	Duo	Brown	USA	White
Dominique	Duo	Brown	USA	Black/White
Dorking	Duo	White	United Kingdom	Multi
Favaucana	Egg	Green	USA	Salmon
Faverolles	Duo	Light Brown	France	Salmon

Fayoumi	Egg	Off White	Egypt	Gold, Silver
Holland	Duo	White	USA	White
Japanese Bantam	Show	Brown	Japan	Multi
Lincolnshire Buff	Duo	Tinted	United Kingdom	Buff
Marans	Egg	Dark Brown	France	Black/Multi
Orpington	Meat	Pinkish Brown	United Kingdom	Buff/Multi
Plymouth Rock	Duo	Tinted	USA	Black/White
Silkie Bantam	Egg	Pale Cream	Asia	Multi
Sussex	Duo	Light Brown	United Kingdom	Brown/ Multi
Welsummer	Duo	Dark Brown	Holland	Partridge
Wyandotte	Duo	Light Brown	USA	Black/ White/Multi

Readers scoring mostly 6's on the chicken style mini-quiz (p. 9) this list is for you:

\ Quick Guide to Endangered Chickens				
BREED	**TYPE**	**EGG COLOR**	**ORIGIN**	**FEATHER COLOR**
Campine	Egg	White	Belgium	Gold, Silver
Chantecler	Duo	Light Brown	Canada	White
Crevecoeur	Duo	White	France	Black, Blue, White
Derbyshire Redcap	Duo	White	United Kingdom	Red, Black
Holland	Duo	White	USA	White
Modern Game	Game	White	United Kingdom	Multi
Nankin	Show	Tinted	Asia	Buff
Russian Orloff	Show	Tinted	Russia	Black, Mahogany, White
Spanish	Egg	White	Mediterranean	Black
Sultan	Show	White	Turkey	White
Sumatra	Show	White	Asia	Black, Blue, White
Yokohama	Show	White	Japan	Multi

Chick Tip: Endangered chickens, as their name implies, can be more challenging to rear. You may need a little more time and patience to nurture them, but your efforts will be rewarding—you are helping the breed to survive!

In addition to raising endangered breeds for their intended purpose (i.e., show, egg, meat), consider breeding the chickens to further ensure their long-term survival. For complete lists of critical or threatened breeds and breeds "under watch" for extinction, consult the Livestock Conservatory (livestockconservancy.org).

LIFESTYLES OF THE RICH AND LUXURIOUS CHICKEN COOP

Your glamorous flock deserves opulent digs, but, more importantly, the resident coop needs to provide a comfortable and functional environment. Pampering and keeping your chickens happy in their new home will reward you with healthy, productive birds.

Whether you choose to design your own lavish chicken condo or purchase a manufactured coop, there are basic criteria that must be met. Layout, space, location, and intent (eggs, meat, breeding, or show) are all important considerations when selecting a dream home.

FIVE QUESTIONS YOU NEED TO ASK BEFORE CHOOSING A CHICKEN COOP

1. **How many chickens will you keep?**

For each chicken in your coop, a minimum of eight to ten square feet will be required to keep your flock content if you do not have a chicken run. If you are raising smaller chickens, like Bantams, the square footage can be reduced to six to seven square feet per chicken. If you plan to have an outdoor run (or free range) for your chickens, then four to six square feet of housing per chicken will suffice for most breeds.

Space is not something that should be compromised. Chickens in too close quarters will be stressed, may have health problems, and may develop "picking" habits, meaning they will pluck feathers from the other chickens. Picking is an awfully hard habit to break your chickens of once it has started!

If you are dealing with limited space, such as raising chickens on an apartment rooftop or in a small backyard setting, your space allocation will dictate how many chickens you may successfully raise and what style of chicken will best thrive. In confined spaces, breeding is not a viable option. Small coops are best suited for show, meat, or egg laying chickens.

Also, plan ahead when thinking about space requirements. You may be starting with ten chicks, but if your intent is to breed the chickens, you'll soon need extra space for your growing family.

2. What is your climate?

If you live in a colder climate, a larger coop will be a necessity. Even if your chickens are free-range or have a large run, if you plan to confine them during extreme temperatures, they'll need the extra space.

Insulation may be a consideration as well. Having an insulated coop is not a necessity and in fact can be a hindrance in warmer climates, as it will encourage moisture and mold. In colder climates, it may be necessary to weatherize the coop in winter months, so the ability to insulate will be of importance when selecting the best housing.

3. Will you free-range your chickens?

If you plan to allow chickens to roam your land or backyard freely, you'll need to give special consideration to doors and fencing. Free-range chickens will need to be secured at night and set free in the morning. An automatic door design may be a great asset when you are not available to perform these tasks.

Fencing of four to six feet in height may be needed to constrict the range of the chickens—for example, if you wish to keep them from tearing up the tomatoes in your garden. Free-range chickens will also be vulnerable to predators, and fencing may be needed to keep them out of wooded areas or from roaming too far.

You may also wish to consider having a coop with an attached chicken run to give the chickens the best of both worlds: the cozy coop and the large free-range area. Runs help keep chickens safe from predators, will not need to be closed up at night or opened in the morning, and are considered to be the lowest-maintenance option.

The drawback to having a chicken run is that chickens will quickly eat through vegetation inside the run. Mobile designs, commonly referred to as "chicken tractors," which include a coop and a run that are easily moved from one spot to the next with the aid of wheels, may be a solution. This type of coop allows chickens to graze alternate areas of ground on a regular basis. Another solution is to use a paddock system to shut off areas of the chicken yard. Chickens are allowed to deplete one section, then are moved to the next while the first area is replenished...and so on.

4. What type of chickens will you be raising?

Will you be raising chickens for eggs, meat, rescue, show, or a combination of purposes? At a minimum, all chickens will need roosts—a perch or ledge for them to sleep on at night. Ideally, roosts are located high off the ground, so the height of your chicken coop is a factor to consider. While a roost that is a minimum of one foot from the bottom of the coop is acceptable, most breeds prefer higher roosts. On the roost, an eight-to-ten-inch space per bird is preferable.

Chickens may roost high, but they nest low. However, not all chickens will need a nesting box. If you do not have laying hens, you can skip this component. If you do have layers, nesting boxes will be a necessity. Without them, your hens will lay eggs everywhere (and trust me—they can be hard to find!). The best rule of thumb is to have one nesting box per four chickens.

 Chick Tip: If you are designing your own coop, empty wooden wine cases with the slots removed make excellent nesting boxes. Cardboard boxes may also be used, but will require constant replacement.

Other important factors in deciding what style of coop to build or purchase are:

- **Ventilation**: A good ventilation system will prevent dust, ammonia from droppings, and moisture from building up, which is essential to your brood's health.
- **Cleaning**: Droppings will need to be removed regularly. A structure that allows for easy entry will be a blessing!

- **Feeding**: A designated feeding spot for your chickens will help keep your coop tidy and dissuade your chickens from using the spot for roosting or laying eggs. Feeding areas need to be clear of roosts or well-covered to avoid droppings from contaminating the water or food.
- **Egg Collection**: If you are raising egg chickens, a coop with a five-foot roof or higher will make it much easier for you to collect eggs daily.
- **Position of Roost**: One of the most common flaws in design is having the roosts directly above the nesting boxes. Chickens will expel waste at night. If the coop is not large enough to set the roosts away from the nesting boxes, a shallow bin with a wire mesh cover will be needed to collect the waste for ease of removal.
- **Pecking Order**: The social structure of your chickens is known as the pecking order. The highest perches in the coop will typically be claimed by the birds highest in the pecking order. It's very common to find roosters on the highest roost. To support your chickens' natural tendencies, incorporate roosts of varying heights into the design. A ladder design is a great style.
- **Position of Nesting Boxes**: If nesting boxes are placed too high in the coop, the chickens may confuse them with roosts. It's more convenient for egg collection to have higher nesting boxes, but you will find yourself having to clean out droppings regularly if the chickens use them as roosts during the night.
- **Protection from the Elements**. Chickens need a place to escape the rain and sun. Some chicken coop designs are raised off the ground, leaving a nice hiding place underneath. Coops with runs generally allow the chickens to roam freely in and out of the coop. Another design consideration is to have the chicken coop sheltered by trees to help protect it from the elements. However you decide to design it, do have a designated area to help protect your flock.
- **Dusting Areas**. If you have a very small space to work with and do not plan to free-range your chickens, keep in mind that chickens need a dusting area. A dusting area is basically a dry patch of ground where the chickens will use the soil to clean their feathers; this is how chickens bathe. A dust box measuring a minimum of one foot deep by one foot wide by two feet long will give a chicken adequate room to dust. Dust boxes should not be kept near feed or water or directly under a roost.

- **Hatching Chicks**: If you plan to hatch chicks or breed chickens, your coop will also need to be baby chick-friendly, with ample room to allow the newborns to grow. You may also need accessible electricity for growing lamps and special feeders for chicks.

RAISING BABY CHICKS LIKE A ROCK STAR

Paparazzi (aka everyone you know, including you) will be prone to smother your baby chicks with adoration. In truth, they're hard to resist! So cute, soft, fluffy, and cuddly—baby chicks are truly endearing, but just like any celebrity, they require some serious coddling.

Baby chicks may be purchased by mail order, from local farmers, farm supply stores or hatcheries. Ideally, begin with at least three chicks, however, keep in mind that many hatcheries will not sell less than twenty-five chicks per order, and local farm stores may require a purchase of six to twelve. If you only have room for a smaller number, consider splitting an order with a friend or neighbor who is interested in raising chickens.

 Chick Tip: When you're purchasing baby chicks, it helps to know the terminology. Pullets are hens. Cockerels are male chickens. A straight run is a mixed-sex lot of chickens.

If you prefer to hatch baby chicks, you will find that there are three incubators capable of hatching eggs: a broody hen, a forced-air incubator, or a still-air incubator. Broody hens are the biggest divas in the chicken yard, but of course nature is the best when it comes to hatching.

Hens become broody when they are ready to begin sitting to hatch eggs. They will remain in the nesting box and get highly defensive if disturbed. Now is the time all good paparazzi know to stay away unless they want their cameras pecked! A hen will sit for twenty-one days, turning the eggs several times per day and generally leaving them once per day to eat and drink.

If you opt to begin with a broody hen, nature will take its course. Your most important role will be to ensure the hen has sufficient water and food nearby, letting her do the rest. If the hen does not have access to the outdoors, where she could normally wet herself with dew, the eggs may need a little additional help from you. During the last week of incubation, the eggs will need to have a sprinkle of warm water each day. The best time to do this is while the hen is busy feeding.

If you have an unmotherly breed of chicken with no broody hens, or if you decide to introduce chickens to your home by hatching, follow these tenets to ensure your success in hatching healthy chicks:

GUIDELINES FOR RAISING A ROCK-STAR CHICK

1. **You must have star power.**

The "it" factor is highly important to the success of your incubation efforts. If you want to raise a little brood of talent, you must begin with good-quality, fresh-laid, fertile eggs. If you are establishing chickens for the first time, the best sources to find eggs are local farm stores, hatcheries or poultry farmers.

2. **You must provide a decked-out pad.**

Having an incubator is still not as good as having a broody hen, but it is a viable option if you invest in quality materials and tend to the eggs well. The two types of home incubators available are forced-air incubators and still-air incubators.

Forced-Air Incubator	Still-Air Incubator
Contains a built-in fan to circulate air	Does not contain a built-in fan
Air flow is regulated	Air flow is not regulated
Larger in size and capacity	Smaller in size and capacity
More expensive	Less expensive

If you are brand-new to incubating eggs and are not certain you will continue, choose a still-air incubator. If you are planning to incubate eggs regularly or would like a high success rate, investing in a forced-air incubator is a good decision.

Regardless of what incubator selection you make, the unit needs to be set up on a flat surface that has accessibility to an electric outlet, and is free of drafts, out of direct sunlight, and not located near heating sources like vents or radiators.

3. You must not wash the eggs.

If there are any dirty spots on the eggs and you feel it is a necessity to remove them, rub gently with a dry cloth.

4. You should make your mark.

Most incubators require hand turning of the eggs. Eggs should be turned a minimum of three times per day for the first eighteen days of the twenty-one-day hatching period; for the last three days, the eggs should be left to rest. Marking the eggs gently with a soft pencil will help you remember which way to turn them.

Some incubator models have a built-in turner, but the small marks will still help you, especially in determining if the turning function is working properly.

5. You should set up a recording studio.

A notepad is an easy way to track how many times you've turned the eggs and in which direction you turned them. It's also handy for recording temperatures and humidity levels and for counting down the days of incubation.

6. You must follow the lead.

Each incubator will come with a specific set of instructions that should be followed. If the correct temperature and humidity levels are not achieved, the chicks will not hatch. Ideal settings for incubators are temperatures of 100 degrees Fahrenheit and a humidity of 60 percent, but each incubator will have its own requirements to achieve optimum levels. For example, many still-air incubators may require a higher temperature of 103 degrees Fahrenheit for successful hatching.

7. You must not interfere with the chick's career.

A common newbie mistake is to try to hurry along the hatching process, as new chicken owners can mistake slow hatching for distress. Do not help the chick to hatch. It may take a baby chick twenty-four hours to emerge from the shell; this is perfectly normal and the process should not be interfered with.

8. **You must remember not all eggs will make it to stardom.**
Despite your best efforts, not all eggs will hatch. When the egg does not hatch or the chick dies at birth, it is heartbreaking, but is also part of nature's design when you've done everything you can to hatch the egg properly.

At the two-week mark of the incubation period, you will be able to determine if the egg is fertile and growing by using a candling method. Candling an egg is holding the egg in front of a bright light, such as a candle or flashlight, in a darkened room. If the egg is clear with no shadow or sign of a chicken forming, it should be removed from the incubator.

9. **You must keep the crib clean.**
Prior to and between incubation periods, the incubator should be washed and sterilized to provide the best hatching environment possible for the newborns.

Newborn chicks should be left in the incubator for at least twelve to twenty-four hours, or until they are dry and their feathers are fluffy. Once they are dry, the baby chicks should be moved to a brooder.

GETTING YOUR ROCK-STAR CHICKS READY FOR THE TOUR

Newborn chicks will need food and water within twenty-four to thirty-six hours after hatching. If you have hatched the chicks with a broody hen, you'll need to leave water and chick crumbs (feed) near the nesting box for the mother to offer. You may wish to set up a box for the hen and her chicks to help keep them comfortable.

Alternatively, you may wish to simply segment off a portion of the chicken coop for the hen to have adequate space and little interference in rearing her brood. When the baby chicks begin moving about the coop, designate an area to hold drinkers and feeders suitable for baby chicks.

If you have used an incubator to hatch the chicks, you will need to set up a brooder box to raise them in. Brooder boxes are available for purchase, but a simple large cardboard box or plastic storage container will work nicely for this purpose.

Set up the brooder box in an area that is free from drafts, is not located near a heat source such as a vent or radiator, and has access to electricity. You may set up a brooder box in a chicken coop, but it's often easier to set it up in your home. Plus you'll have the added advantage of being able to keep a closer eye on the chicks and to enjoy their soft, fluffy-cute chickness—which will not last long! After four to five weeks, the baby chicks will fly the brooder box and begin their tour of the coop.

In addition to the brooder box, you will need bedding, shallow food and water containers, chick crumbs, and a heat source. A low-hanging light bulb will provide adequate heat. A clip-on style will make it easy to position the light and adjust the temperature.

Follow these simple steps to set up your brooder:
- Line the bottom of the brooder box with shredded newspaper, then cover the paper with a layer of paper towel.
- Set up a feeding area with a shallow chick feeder and a water dish. Hanging feeders and water dishes are a great choice as they can easily be raised off the ground as the chicks grow.
- Attach a clip-on lamp or set a hanging lamp with a 250-watt bulb directly above the brooder box. Avoid hanging the light over the feed.
- If you have other pets, place a mesh screen on top of the brooder box to keep curious critters from interfering with your baby chicks.

When you introduce your chicks to the brooder box, you may need to make regular adjustments to your heat source. If the chicks scatter away from the light, it's too warm. If they huddle directly under the light, your brooder box is too cold. Happy, warm chicks will roam around the brooder box freely without showing signs of being too hot or cold.

Initially, you may need to guide your chicks to the food and water you have provided. This can be done by gently moving them and dipping their beaks in the water or feed. Use a starter grower feed for chicks and always use room-tempera-ture water. There are other feed options available for baby chicks, but, if this is your first experience hatching chicks, starter feed will ensure that the baby chicks have the nutrients they need to mature and maintain good health. Starter feed is available at local farm stores and by mail order and is now often found at pet stores and major retailers.

Bedding in the brooder box should be cleaned and changed daily. After the first week, the paper towel layer will not be necessary, and you may switch to shredded newspaper only or to other bedding materials, such as sand.

The primary health concerns of baby chicks are pasting, coccidiosis, and pneu-monia:

- **Pasting** is when droppings adhere to the chick's bottom and form a "paste" that seals the opening. To correct, moisten the droppings and gently rub them off with a damp towel.
- **Coccidiosis** is a parasitic disease of the intestinal tract. Consistent watery droppings are a sign of this infection. To prevent, keep the roosting box clean by changing water and bedding frequently.
- **Pneumonia** is a respiratory infection caused by damp living conditions. To prevent, change bedding frequently and wipe up any water spills promptly.

If you find that you have a sick baby chick, it is best to give the chick its own small brooder box or to portion off a section of your large brooder box that can be accessed only by the chicken that has fallen ill. Isolating the chick will keep it from infecting the other baby chicks and will keep them from pecking the weaker chick. This will also allow you to pamper the chick and hopefully nurse it back to proper health.

In the event that a baby chick dies, it must be removed from the brooder imme-diately and disposed of properly by either burial or burning.

After four to five weeks of confinement in the brooder box, your baby chicks will be well on their way to adult stardom and may be moved to the coop. Around this time, the chicks will begin roosting and will need low perches for this purpose.

If you do not provide a few perches, the chicks may be tempted to use nesting houses or their feeders!

At eighteen weeks, your baby chicks will be full-fledged rock stars and are ready to transition to adult chicken feed. Feed may differ for layers versus meat birds, so consult the feed section in the next chapter and research your breed's particular needs.

At around nineteen to twenty-five weeks, chickens may have some confusion over nesting boxes versus roosts, especially if there are no older chickens to show them the ropes. You may need to hand-place chickens on roosting areas at night until they get the hang of it.

At around twenty to twenty-four weeks, hens will begin laying eggs.

If you need help with your young brood, a fabulous resource is Biosecurity for Birds, from the USDA's Animal and Plant Health Inspection Service, which offers guidance for backyard poultry producers: www.aphis.usda.gov/animal_health/birdbiosecurity.

3. Get Fowl:

Caring for Your Chickens

FINE DINING FOR PAMPERED CHICKS

Every meal in your chicken coop needs to begin with the best refreshments. Agua, water, H_2O—whatever you choose to call it, chickens need plenty of it! If chickens do not have an adequate supply of clean, fresh water at all times, they will not produce quality eggs, will have stunted growth, will be stressed, and will ultimately suffer health-wise. Your chickens need much more water than they do feed, particularly in the summer (or hot) months. In the winter months, you may need a water heater to keep the H_2O flowing. Bottom line: a well-watered chicken is an exceptionally happy chicken.

As the master chef for your chickens, your meal prep and serve time will be dictated by the daylight hours. Chickens eat constantly and need plenty of food at their peck and call. When a chicken matures to adult feed, dietary options broaden, and you will be able to provide a veritable feast for your fowl.

If you wish to stick to commercially available feed, it's certainly an acceptable diet choice and your chickens will thrive. Various formulas are available for layers, breeders, meat chickens, and general all-purpose feed.

If you wish to add more variety, your kitchen, container gardens, or backyard will provide a wide range of culinary options that will enhance your chickens' health by providing natural health benefits, remedies, nutrients, and proteins. On average, a healthy, mature chicken will eat around two pounds of feed per week. When you consider the cost of commercial feed, it's also a monetary saving to use natural resources to supplement your chickens' diet.

Free-range chickens will self-feed seed, insects, and plants. They need no instructions and will naturally balance their own diet. Simply allow the chickens to forage during the day, then supplement with hand-feeding in the late afternoon. If you live in a seasonal climate, your free-range fowl will have slim pickings in the winter months and hence will require more hand-feeding during that time.

Chickens who are kept in small runs or do not have access to forage will require a constant supply of feed, which can be set up in the morning and again in the late afternoon. There are many different theories on the best time to feed chickens, but one constant, feeding about an hour prior to nightfall, encourages morning egg production—an amazing advantage when it comes to collecting eggs on a schedule.

Hanging feeders and waterers are desirable for keeping chickens well-fed. They keep the food and water at an ideal height for access and help keep it clean and free of droppings. Automatic feeders and waterers are a terrific asset if there are times of the day you may not be able to keep close watch on water and feed supplies.

Chickens will also gladly eat feed off the ground. If you do not have free-range chickens, allow them to forage for feed from the ground inside a short run to keep them more active.

Extra supplies of chicken feed should be kept in a cool, dry, dark spot in an airtight container. This will not only discourage the chickens from getting into the feed but also keep out other pets and predators like field mice.

WOULD YOU LIKE GRITS WITH THAT?

If you've ever traveled south past the Mason-Dixon Line, you'll commonly find grits served up with every meal. It's not the same dish, but chickens need grit with their meals too, even free-range chickens who may not find enough supply in the soil. Grit allows a chicken to grind food in its gizzard (often referred to a second stomach) in somewhat the same manner as we grind food with our teeth.

Keep a supply of grit in an accessible container for your chickens to utilize when needed. Ground oyster shells are an excellent choice of grit for layers; they add calcium to the hen's diet, which in turn helps produce a nice strong shell for eggs. If you are raising primarily male chickens, opt for a granite grit, as too much calcium may have an adverse effect on roosters.

Grit is often confused with scratch by new chicken owners. Scratch, a treat typically made up of cracked corn, is not a necessary component of a chicken's diet. Basically, scratch is like dessert for chickens and is generally used for training chickens or for adding a little fuel and fat to chickens who may need extra warmth in harsh winters.

DOES THAT BOWL FULL OF OATS MAKE ME LOOK FAT?

Beyond basic feed, chickens will enjoy and thrive on diets supplemented with gourmet goods like grains, bugs, worms, vegetables, fruits, chopped greens, milk, and table scraps. Favorites include tomatoes, lettuce, sprouts, apple parings, carrot tops, Swiss chard, overripe vegetables and fruits, peapods, and toast crumbs. If you happen to have stale whole-grain cereal with a low sugar content that you want to dispose of, your chickens will go gaga over this simple treat.

Keep in mind that what you put into a chicken's diet is what you will get out. If you choose less healthy options, you'll have less than desirable results, and your bird's health may suffer as a result. Well-fed hens produce more eggs, but balanced feed produces the healthiest eggs. Well-fed chickens produce more meat, but balanced feed produces the healthiest, leanest meat.

Some food should be given very sparingly. For example, chickens love corn, but corn is high-fat and low-protein. Fat hens are not good layers. Other foods are healthy as can be—such as green peppers, cabbage, and citrus fruits—but your chickens may turn up their beaks at them.

Chickens have a primary need for protein in their diet, and outside of commercial feed the best sources are worms, grubs, bugs, milk, butcher scraps, sunflower seeds, and alfalfa. Hens and baby chicks need plenty of calcium, which can be supplemented through items like milk, scratch, greens, and squash blossoms.

Another way to help add calcium to your hens' diet is to feed them ground eggshells. After using eggs for cooking, rinse, dry, and crush the shells, then mix them into the hens' daily feed.

Chickens with low exposure to natural light—in winter or in low-light coops—may need additional vitamin D. Hens will produce very thin eggshells if vitamin D resources are low. Fish oil, cod oil, sardines, and milk added to the diet will help provide supplies of this important vitamin.

Even if your chickens are on a full commercial feed diet, there are still natural ingredients you may wish to consider adding to their feed to help keep your flock in tip-top shape or to address particular health concerns. Use this chart as a handy reference:

Natural Feed Supplements for Chickens	
BREWER'S YEAST	Helpful in preventing lice and mite infestations. Add 1 teaspoon per chicken to daily feed.
COMFREY	Helpful with worm prevention. Add a small amount to feed occasionally.
CIDER VINEGAR	Helpful with overall health. Add 1 Tbsp. to water regularly.
CUT MINT	Helpful in repelling lice and ticks. Add a small amount to feed occasionally.
DANDELIONS	Helpful with overall health and adding calcium to diet. Add to feed regularly.
FENNEL	Helpful with overall health. Add seeds and foliage to feed regularly
FLAXSEED	Helpful in adding protein to diet and boosting Omega 3's in eggs. Add a small amount to feed regularly.
GARLIC	Helpful with overall health and worm prevention. Add a small amount of crushed garlic occasionally to feed or water.

LAVENDER	Helpful in repelling lice. Add dried lavender to dust baths and plant lavender around chicken coops.
MARIGOLD	Helpful with skin health. Also brightens egg yolks. Add to feed regularly.
NASTURTIUM	Helpful with de-worming. Add leaves and flowers to diet if worms are detected.
ROSEMARY	Helpful in repelling insects. Add to feed on occasion and plant around chicken coop area.
SAGE	Helpful with overall health. Add to feed regularly.
SQUASH BLOSSOMS	Helpful in adding calcium to diet. Add fresh blossoms to feed occasionally.
SUNFLOWER SEEDS	Helpful in adding protein to diet. Add to feed regularly.
TANSY	Helpful with worm prevention. Add a small amount to feed occasionally.
WORMWOOD	Helpful with worm prevention and repelling insects. Add to feed on occasion and plant around the chicken coop area.

 Chick Tip: Grow oat sprouts in the winter to supplement your chickens' needs for fresh greens. Find a recipe for sprouting oats in Chapter 4 (Get Dirty).

HOW TO AVOID BAD MEAL REVIEWS

The most important thing every chef catering to chickens needs to know is that chickens will eat nearly everything! This includes cat and dog food, grapes, and your favorite roses. Chickens are naturally curious, so you do need to be mindful of their surroundings and not place harmful objects in their path.

Many common things can be harmful or toxic to chickens. Among them are screws, Styrofoam, treated seeds, and potato peels. "Toxic" does not always indicate that the substance is fatal to your chicken, but it can cause anything from mild irritation to fatality and is therefore best avoided.

There's no need to completely rid your property of all foliage. Well-fed and cared-for chickens will not be prone to forage through most plants around your yard, including herbs, but there are foods that should not be fed to your chicken or left where they will have access to. Use this list to help keep your chickens safe from harmful substances:

Common Plants, Foods and Substances That May Be Harmful or Toxic To Chickens		
Alcohol	Amaryllis	Antifreeze
Avocado	Azalea	Bird of Paradise
Boxwood	Bracken Fern	Bulb Flowers
Cacao	Caffeinated food or drinks	Cat Food
Coffee (Senna)	Coffee Beans	Coral Plant
Coriander	Cutleaf Philodendron	Daffodil
Dog Food	Eggplant	Elephant Ear
English Ivy	Eucalyptus (dried)	Foxglove
Fried Foods	Gasoline	Hemlock
Holly	Honeysuckle	Horse Chestnut
Horse Tail	Hyacinth	Hydrangea
Jasmine	Juniper	Lily of the Valley
Marijuana	Mexican Poppy	Milkweed
Mistletoe (dried)	Morning Glory	Mountain Laurel

Mushrooms	Nettles	Nightshades
Oak (and acorns)	Oleander	Peace Lily
Periwinkle	Pesticides	Philodendrons
Poinsettia	Poison Ivy	Poison Oak
Potatoes	Rape (Rapeseed)	Red Sage
Rhubarb Leaves	Rodent Poison	Small Machine Parts or Tools
Sorghum	Spoiled or Rotten Food	Styrofoam
Sweet Pea	Tobacco	Wisteria

Also be careful about feeding chickens fish, garlic and onions. They are not known toxins, but they will add flavor—often unwanted—to your eggs. A hint of garlic in your scrambled eggs is splendid, but in your vanilla cupcakes it is not a welcome addition!

HANG ON A MINUTE, THIS ONE DIDN'T COME WITH INSTRUCTIONS

The key to having tame chickens is to get them accustomed to your touch from the time they are baby chicks. If you regularly pick them up gently, feed them from your hand (gloves can be used), pet them, gently carry them around for a few minutes, and talk or sing softly to them, the chickens will quickly learn to respond positively to your presence.

Despite your best efforts to tame them, roosters can become aggressive, particularly older roosters. It's always a good idea to keep small children away from chickens and never leave children unattended near your flock. If a rooster becomes regularly aggressive, quite frankly, it may be time to make stew of it.

First, be certain to check your own actions to ensure you didn't force the rooster into an aggressive state. Did you corner the rooster or rush toward it in a demanding manner? Did he perceive you as a threat in any way? Roosters are instinctively protective. To defuse the aggressive rooster, you can quickly offer some feed or sometimes, better yet, pick the rooster up to subdue and hold him to show him who is boss and also who cares for him.

Do not mistake adoration for aggression. If you are the primary feeder of your chickens, you may find that roosters and hens regularly rush at you when they spot you. They are not looking for a fight; they are looking for food! When a rooster feels threatened, he will generally not speed toward you right away. The rooster will do a little dance, fluffing its feathers, possibly scratching at the ground with one foot, and then race forward to attack.

Alternatively, roosters can be fully tamed by turning them into capons. Capons are roosters that have been castrated. The process is intense and expensive, though, and the only advantage is that the rooster, now capon, will become significantly larger, producing a higher meat yield.

CATCH THEM IF YOU CAN

Catching a chicken, especially if you have not tamed your flock, can be an entertaining challenge. If you've never tried, the first time may leave you a bit breathless and befuddled as to how quickly your chick can move. Do not give up. If you attempt to catch a chicken and then give up, you will have taught it how to successfully evade you.

Chickens can sense your discomfort and are easily startled. Whether you plan to pick your chickens up or not, whenever you walk into the chicken yard or the general vicinity of your chickens, remain calm. Walk slowly, use slow movements, and avoid making loud noises. The more time you spend with and around your chickens, the less frightened they will be.

If you have constantly handled the chickens from the time they were baby chicks, you should have a relatively easy time simply walking over to a particular chicken and picking it up. If you think you will have significant trouble picking up one of your chickens but have an urgent need to, such as to separate a sick chicken from the flock, wait until nightfall. Once the chicken has roosted and fallen asleep, simply pick it up off the roost and relocate it.

Poultry nets are handy if you have a wild flock that has not been handled often, if you will be butchering chickens, or if you're simply a little shy about picking up your full-grown chickens. Nets are available by mail order or may be found at local farm stores.

When you pick up your chicken, your primary concern will be to secure its legs and wings. Wrap one hand around the middle of the chicken to gently bind the wings to its body, and wrap your other hand gently around the chicken's legs. When a chicken's movements are restricted, it will typically settle down quickly. Help soothe the chicken by talking softly to it, petting it or gently stroking the back of its neck area. Unless you are confident that your chicken has been well tamed, try to keep your head or other exposed parts of your body away from the chicken's head as it may attempt to peck you.

Regardless of what you may have seen in movies or in photos, do not carry a chicken by its neck or wings. You may damage the fowl (and yourself) in the process. Carrying a chicken upside down by its legs is also risky. The chicken may struggle, and, if you lose your grip, injuries can result.

EGGS, GLORIOUS EGGS

Hens begin laying eggs about twenty to twenty-four weeks after hatching and will lay regularly, with consistency in amount, size, and shape, by twenty-seven to thirty weeks. A hen will typically lay for seven to ten years and may live to age ten to fourteen. Egg production will be at its highest peak the first year and then steadily decrease with each laying season. Prime seasons are considered to be laying years one through four.

For a steady amount of eggs, you'll need to add new hens to the flock every year at a 1:4 ratio, meaning that once per year one new hen should be introduced to the flock for every four layers already in production.

Chickens will not stop laying eggs in the winter unless you are in an area with extreme temperatures. Even then, if the coop has been weather-proofed or tempera-ture regulated, the hen may continue to lay despite the frigid temperatures outside.

A hen normally spends around twenty-four hours forming an egg prior to hatching it. To encourage egg production and prevent broody hens, collect eggs regularly at the same time each day—unless, of course, you are intent on breeding your chickens! Leaving an egg each day or a using a wooden egg prop in nesting boxes will help encourage your hens to lay in the same spot. Be sure to lightly mark the egg that you leave behind with a pencil so you can collect it the next day to prevent spoilage.

Eggs will vary dramatically in size and color depending upon the breed, from whites, tans, and pinks to blues, greens, and reddish-browns. A single hen's eggs will also vary a bit in size and color depending upon her diet. Occasionally, eggs will have a double yolk, a speck of blood, or a white or dark speck when you crack them open. These are all normal. A tiny white or dark speck will often be an indicator that the egg was fertilized. Some people prefer to remove this dot prior to cooking, but it is not hazardous to your diet.

The egg is inedible if it contains a partially developed chick, if it is spoiled, or if it is cracked. At this point, it is best to dispose of or to compost the egg.

Occasionally, eggs collected will be dirty or have droppings adhered to the shell. It is not a good idea to wash the egg, as the egg has a naturally protective barrier. You need to keep this barrier in place to keep bacteria out. Instead, gently buff the egg with a clean, dry towel until the dirt or droppings are removed prior to storage.

On average, eggs can be stored for up to six weeks if refrigerated properly. If you find a random egg that was laid outside of the nesting box or question whether an egg is fresh enough for use, a simple water test will help reveal if it is fit for consumption.

DIY: EGG-FRESHNESS WATER TEST

Fill a medium saucepan with room-temperature water. Place the egg in question gently into the pan.

If the egg is fresh, it will lie at the bottom of the bowl. If the egg is a few days to a week old, one end of the egg will tilt upward. If the egg is a week old or more, the egg will stand upright on one end. If the egg is spoiled (and not fit for consumption), it will float.

WHAT ABOUT DUAL-PURPOSE OR MEAT CHICKENS?

You may be raising chickens for meat purposes, or it may be the end of your egg chicken's prime production cycle. In both cases, the chicken will need to be properly butchered and de-feathered. There are plenty of materials (books, videos, blogs) available offering guidance on humane slaughter techniques; however, it is best to consult an expert and receive hands-on instruction for your first efforts. Contact your local county extension agency for support and referrals. Alternatively, for a small sum, many butchers and chicken farmers offer services.

HEALTHY-CHICKEN CODES DECODED

My hen looks constipated. Is that for real?

Hens can develop pasting, as referenced in the baby chick section of Chapter 2 (Get Laid). However, it's more likely that your hen is egg-bound. When a hen is egg-bound, her cavity is dry (common in older hens) or the egg for some other reason, like poor diet, is unable to pass through the vent. The hen will squat and strain in a manner that resembles constipation. She may also be lethargic and appear to be sick. When a hen is egg-bound, it is a life-threatening condition.

There are many methods and theories on how to coax an egg from an egg-bound hen. Above all, it is first best to consult a veterinarian. To help the hen, set her in a warm bath for 15 minutes. After removing her from the bath, apply room-temperature lubricant (e.g., KY Jelly) or a little warm olive oil to the hen's vent to help coax the egg out. The hen must be treated within twenty-four to forty-eight hours, or the end result will be her death.

Help! My chicken has a broken leg!

Broken legs are more common in baby chicks than in adult chickens, but both traumas are handled in the same manner. The broken leg can be splinted with a small, flat stick, like a clean Popsicle stick, and wrapped and tied into place with gauze. Tape may be used but could cause damage to the chicken's skin when removed. The bird should be isolated from the flock until the broken limb heals.

If any bones protrude from the break, it is best to consult a veterinarian.

Why is my chicken losing feathers?

Most chickens molt once a year, typically in fall or early winter. Hens will quit laying during molting, and roosters will quit breeding. The birds will lose old feathers, which will be replaced by new. Once the molting period has ended, hens will begin laying eggs again and roosters will be interested in breeding. On average, molting lasts one to four months. Feeding your chickens plenty of greens during this time may speed up the process a bit. If you have clipped your chicken's wings to keep it from flying, you will need to do so again after the new feathers replace the old.

Why does my chicken have bloody feathers?

Bloody feathers on a chicken are most likely a sign that the chicken is infested with lice or mites. It can also be an indicator that the chicken is being pecked on by other fowl. Sadly, chicken cannibalism can happen.

Seriously? Chicken cannibalism? How does that happen?

Chickens can fall into practices ranging from feather- or toe-picking other chickens to a full-on attack on their flesh, referred to as chicken cannibalism. When a chicken is picked on by other fowl, it's generally a sign of overcrowding in the coop. This behavior may also be due to a nutrient deficiency in the offending chicken's diet, such as a lack of protein, salt, or calcium. Adjusting or supplementing feed may cure the behavior.

This behavioral habit is hard to break, once established, even if the dietary concerns are corrected. You may need to separate the offending chicken from the flock and check and adjust her diet; then reintroduce her to the flock once she seems to be well adjusted. It is possible, though, that the offending chicken may need to be culled.

Occasionally, an injury on the chicken who is being picked on is the cause. In this case, the coop will need to be checked for sharp edges and protruding nails or wood that may need to be corrected.

If chicken cannibalism is present in the brooder among baby chicks, it is most often a sign that the temperature is too hot, the ventilation is poor, or the brooder house is suffering from poor sanitation.

My bird is sick, what do I do?

If you have a sick bird, immediately isolate it from the flock to prevent the spread of possible infection. If you are unable to determine the cause, consult your local veterinarian, your county extension agency, or a poultry expert to help diagnose and treat the fowl.

How do I know my bird is sick?

Wheezing, whistling noises, lethargy, bloody stools, abnormal growth patterns, and erratic changes in behavior or appearance are all red flags for illness. If illness is suspected, always isolate the chicken and seek expert advice.

I walked into the coop and found one of my chickens had died. What now?

Sudden chicken death can be an indicator of a serious illness, but could also be caused by a toxin, cancer, old age, or natural causes. Unless the other chickens in the flock are exhibiting signs of illness or toxins, it can be truly difficult to diagnose. Remove the dead bird immediately and dispose of it properly through burial or burning. Then simply be extra mindful about inspecting the remaining flock and watching for signs of possible diseases. When in doubt, do not hesitate to consult an expert such as your local veterinarian.

Can my chicken get chicken pox? Should I vaccinate?

Chickens cannot contract the human disease chicken pox, but they can contract a number of other common ailments such as Newcastle disease, which affects their respiratory system. Vaccinations are recommended but may not be necessary for small home flocks. Check with your local veterinarian for vaccines that are commonly administered in your area. The most common vaccinations are for viral infections like bronchitis and are easily administered via the chicken's water supply.

My chicken is sleeping a lot longer than usual. Is this normal?

Chickens roost and sleep by the sun. When the sun goes down, chickens will sleep. In winter when days are shorter, they will sleep more. This is perfectly normal.

Less daylight time, though, does mean less egg production. There are chicken owners who simulate light production, but it's generally best to let the hens follow nature's rhythms and not to mess with artificial lighting. Not to miss mentioning that artificial lighting is expensive in comparison to the end result (increased egg production) and will up your carbon footprint in the process. If you happen to live in an area with excessively long winters or periods of completely dark days, such as areas in Alaska, artificial lighting may be a big benefit throughout the dark season.

If the chicken is lethargic throughout the day and sleeping in daylight, it is an indicator of a more serious problem, probably an illness, and you should consult a veterinarian.

I am totally confused, can't tell one chicken from another. How do I know my old hens from my new?

Initially, it is easy to tell which chickens are which, especially when they are brand-spanking-new, but when you begin introducing new layers to your flock, the hens may begin to blend in, especially if you are staying with one breed. A simple solution is to band your chickens when they are young. Banding is used to help you remember when chickens were hatched so that you can easily differentiate newer chickens from the older ones. Bands are available for purchase by mail order in various sizes by breed.

THE THING ABOUT CHICKENS, PETS, AND GARDENS

You will want your chickens to range free without restrictions. Indeed, it's the best scenario for them, and it's what nature originally intended. But, if your plans also include a well-manicured lawn, flowers, and a big, beautiful vegetable garden, you may need to modify your plans a bit. Chickens have two natural habits that can be detrimental to your landscape and garden: scratching and dusting. If you have lush green grass or bountiful gardens, be aware that chickens can, and likely will, wreak havoc.

On the upside, chickens love to eat bugs! Letting chickens free-range for a restricted time period around your garden and house can dramatically reduce the numbers of ticks, ants, snails, slugs, and other common pests on your property. Fencing can be used to control when the chickens have access to various areas.

It's usually best to keep chickens out of the garden when you are sowing seeds or transplanting new growth. They may accidentally scratch the new seeds or, worse, intentionally dig them up. They enjoy sprouts, so they may also eat new growth. When your garden is producing, chickens may interfere with the growth and may also try to peck bugs off plants or decide to have a taste of your tomatoes.

Chickens will rarely bother established trees, shrubs, or plants, and you can set wire mesh around new trees or plants to protect them. Raised beds are chicken magnets too, as the chicken may think they are ideal dusting spots. Your chickens may consider spots like strawberry beds to be a gourmet meal stop. Ornamental fencing around the beds will generally deter the chicken from exploring them, but wire mesh may be needed to protect plants like strawberries.

Chickens can fly and often do. Even if you have installed a six-foot fence, your chicken can get over it. If you'd rather not have your chickens hopping the garden fence or visiting your neighbors, clipping their wings is a reasonable solution. Contrary to popular beliefs by those outside the chicken-raising world, clipping a chicken's wings is not painful for the chicken. The process entails using shears to trim back the first ten flight feathers of one of the chicken's wings. The bird will then not have the balance needed for flight, but will not be hindered or restricted in any other way.

Clipping does have to be done regularly, about once per year, as feathers molt and are replaced by new ones.

Household pets can also complicate your chickens' free-range capabilities. Chickens will cohabit with cats and dogs, although cats may go after baby chicks and some dogs will consider chickens tasty snacks. Ideally, you should introduce dogs and cats to chickens when they are puppies and kittens so that they are trained properly and will view the chickens as part of your family.

Still, it may be wise to have an enclosed run if you have dogs. Even when they are raised around baby chicks or introduced to the baby chicks as soon as they hatch, dogs may still try to snack on your chickens or will play roughly with them. It is simply in the dog's nature to do so.

Cats and dogs will often eat chicken feed too. You will need to devise a plan to keep the food separated from your pets. Dogs are also known for developing a taste for fresh eggs once they discover them, so another benefit of a fenced-in run is that it will keep your dogs from getting to the eggs before you do!

Once you have a plan to keep your chickens out of the garden, the next step is to design your dream garden. Look to the stars for inspiration as you begin to carve out your dream pattern.

4. Get Dirty:

Growing Your Garden of Eden

Close your eyes and imagine your dream garden. Are you picturing a vast plot with endless perfect rows of bountiful produce thriving and twinkling under the sun like a Milky Way of green? Yeah, me too. Aaah…

When you open your eyes, though, your environment may not match the grandiose scale of your vision. Maybe you have a small backyard or maybe you don't have a patch of land at all, just a tiny balcony overlooking the parking lot of your apartment complex. Modern landscapers need pocketfuls of creativity and oodles of ingenuity to build our dream gardens. While you may not be able to plant a galaxy of greens, you can still cultivate a space that flourishes.

THIS IS THE DAWNING OF THE AGE OF ORGANIC

Organic gardening simply means gardening in harmony with nature, using ecologically safe methods. Sometimes people shy away from organic gardening, as they think it will be a lot more time consuming and their plants won't be as appealing. Both assumptions are myths. True, it may take slightly more time to pick bugs from leaves than to apply chemical pesticides, but the extra muscle power needed provides invaluable benefits for the plants, the earth, and your health. And, plants, like humans, are exceptionally beautiful in their natural state, imperfections and all.

When you begin your organic gardening journey, keep in mind three key criteria when selecting plant varieties:

1. Choose plants that are native or best suited to your growing area for outdoor gardening. Indoor container gardeners have a little more leeway.

2. Start with plants you are familiar with or those your neighbors have had great success with in your area. For example, there are thousands of tomato varieties, but not all will thrive well in your environment, and some may require extra-special care.

3. At first, grow only what you will eat. Starting small will ensure you can pay close attention to what works and what doesn't, making adjustments as needed along the way. If you have immediate plans to can or preserve large bounties, consider purchasing organic vegetables and fruits from your local farmers market or store to supplement your needs.

Best plants for beginners include:

- Aloe Vera
- Asparagus
- Basil
- Beets
- Bell Peppers
- Butterhead Lettuce
- Cherry Tomatoes
- Chives
- Corn

- Cucumbers
- Dwarf Orange Trees
- Garlic
- Green Beans
- Jalapenos
- Kale
- Oregano
- Parsley
- Rosemary

- Sage
- Shallots
- Spinach
- Squash
- Strawberries
- Sunflowers
- Thyme
- Tomatillos
- Tomatoes

For organic gardening, it's also important to have quality organic matter in the soil. This is where your composting efforts will truly pay off! In early spring, prior to tilling the soil, spread a one-inch layer of compost over the soil and turn it under to about six inches in depth. If you are container gardening, add a one-inch layer to the container and gently mix it into the soil a few weeks before you plant.

Other ways to introduce organic matter into the soil are spreading compost in the fall and tilling it under, spreading manure in the fall and tilling it under, and growing cover crops over the winter, then tilling them under in the spring.

SUCCESS DEPENDS UPON THE SEEDS YOU SOW

Local garden retailers, farm-and-seed stores, and online or mail order seed companies are great resources for seed purchases. The number one thing to remember when ordering or purchasing seeds is to shop (and order) early. It is possible for seed varieties to sell out, and you certainly do not want to be waiting on a shipment when the weather is already prime for planting.

A common question today is to ask whether the seed is a GMO. GMO is the acronym for genetically modified organism, a plant (or animal) created through gene-splicing techniques or genetic engineering. Pertaining to gardening, GMOs are plants that do not biologically occur in nature.

GMO plants should not be confused with hybrid plants. Hybrid plants are developed when two varieties or species of plants are cross-pollinated to produce an offspring that contains the best attributes of the parent plants. Hybrids may occur naturally or, more likely, over a series of years in a plant lab setting.

There are very few crops applicable to gardeners or farmers that have GMO varieties available for purchase. Among them are corn, soybeans, squash, and zucchini. If you have concerns about GMO plants and wish to avoid purchasing them accidentally, it's safest to buy untreated heirloom seed varieties from a reputable vendor.

Heirloom seeds are seeds from a particular region or area that have been hand-selected for more than fifty years and have maintained their original characteristics. They are nonhybrid and open-pollinated by insects or wind without human intervention.

The Council for Responsible Genetics (councilforresponsiblegenetics.org) offers a Safe Seed Resource List to help find resources. Each source on the list has pledged to "not knowingly buy, sell, or trade genetically engineered seeds."

GETTING TO KNOW YOUR SEED PACKETS

The information on each seed packet (or catalogue description) is highly valuable in helping you to determine which plants will be the best for your environment and needs. Reading seed packets is actually quite easy once you have the know-how. Use the following chart to navigate them like a pro:

Seed Terminology	
TERM	**MEANING**
Packed Date	The packed date indicates when the seeds were packaged. When purchasing seeds from a store, look for packets with the current year. The date is usually stamped on the packet in year and lot format, such as "2014 LOT F1"
Season Date	The season date is like a freshness date on food: the seeds are best used by this date. The date is typically stamped onto the packet in month and year format with the country of origin, such as "USA 10/14"
Organic	Seeds grown on an organic farm without use of pesticides, and untreated.
Hybrid	Offspring plant that has been cross-pollinated. Commonly marked with F1 (first generation) or F2 (second generation) offspring.

GM	Seeds that are genetically modified.
Heirloom	Open-pollinated seeds from a particular region or area that have been hand-selected for more than fifty years and have maintained their original characteristics.
Open-Pollinated	Seeds that have been open-pollinated but are not necessarily heirloom seeds.
Annual	A plant that lives for one growing season.
Perennial	A plant that lives for more than two years.
Variety	Early and late varieties are useful to extend your growing seasons.
Days to Germination	How long it will take the seed to sprout.
Days to Harvest	Expected time frame when vegetables or fruits will produce or be ready for harvest.
Plant Height	How tall the plant will be when it matures.
Plant Depth	How deep in the soil to plant the seeds.
Plant Spacing	The distance needed between seeds for the plant to grow properly.
Resistant	Indicates that the plant resists all common insects and diseases better than nonresistant plants
Tolerant	Tolerant means the plant has better resistance to some common insects and diseases than nonresistant plants. The package will further indicate which insects and common diseases the plant is resistant to.
Treated	The plant is chemically treated to prevent diseases like soil rot and other fungi.

US Hardiness Zones	Determined by the US Department of Agriculture and often presented as a color-coded map, this is a guide for growing conditions by area. The map helps determine the length of the growing season in your area and whether the seed is ideal for planting in your area.
When to Plant	Date or date range when it is best to start seeds.
Directions/Care	Generally contains information on the plant's needs for sunlight or shade, its water requirements, the best time to fertilize, and whether the plant needs to be staked.
Suggestions	Additional information that will help ensure the success of the plant, including ideal locations, whether the seed is suitable for container gardening, and helpful hints for harvesting.

Another aspect to take into consideration is what time of year you wish to garden. Will you be a summer gardener when the children are home to help, or will you garden all year round to reap the benefits of a continuous supply of fresh vegetables and fruits?

Common Plants by Sowing Season		
SPRING	**SUMMER**	**FALL/WINTER**
Beets	Beets	Beets
Broccoli	Cabbage	Broccoli
Brussels Sprouts	Cantaloupe	Brussels Sprouts
Cabbage	Carrots	Cabbage
Carrots	Corn	Carrots

Common Plants by Sowing Season, continued		
SPRING	**SUMMER**	**FALL/WINTER**
Cauliflower	Cucumbers	Cauliflower
Celery	Eggplant	Garlic
Cherry Tomatoes	Green Beans	Green Beans
Herbs (all)	Herbs (select)	Herbs (all)
Kale	Kale	Kale
Leaf Lettuce	Lettuce (all varieties)	Leaf Lettuce
Mint	Lima Beans	Mustard
Mustard	Marigolds	Potatoes
Onions	Okra	Radish
Peas	Onions	Rhubarb
Potatoes	Parsley	Snow Peas
Radish	Peppers (all varieties)	Spinach
Spinach	Pumpkins	Turnips
Strawberries	Radish	Winter Squash
Turnips	Spinach	
	Summer Squash	
	Sweet Potatoes	
	Tomatillos	
	Tomatoes	
	Watermelon	
	Winter Squash	

Garden themes help maximize your efforts and ensure everything you grow is in tune with your culinary preferences. Here are a few of my favorites.

IRISH GARDEN	Asparagus, bay leaf, carrots, celery, chives, cucumbers, green onions, garlic, horseradish, parsley, parsnip, potatoes, rhubarb, sage, squash, thyme, tomatoes
ITALIAN GARDEN	Arugula, basil, fava beans, fennel, garlic, Italian heirloom tomatoes, onions, oregano, radicchio, red bell peppers, Romano beans, Roma tomatoes, rosemary
EAST ASIAN GARDEN	Bok choy, Chinese cabbage, eggplant, daikon radishes, green onions, snow peas, soybeans, watercress
LATIN GARDEN	Black beans, bell peppers, chili peppers, cilantro, garlic, garlic chives, onions, tomatillos, tomatoes
PIZZA GARDEN	Basil, bell peppers, cherry tomatoes, mushrooms, onions, oregano, rosemary, tomatoes
EDIBLE FLOWER GARDEN	Chives, cornflowers, daylilies, lavender, marigold, nasturtiums, pansies, sage, thyme, violets
SMOOTHIE GARDEN	Blackberries, blueberries, carrots, dwarf citrus trees, kale, mint, raspberries, spinach, strawberries
SALAD GARDEN	Beets, cucumbers, lettuce (all varieties), green onions, mustard, radishes, spinach, sprouts, tomatoes

One of the crucial questions you need to answer is: where will my garden grow?

The ideal luxury garden spot has:
- access to a full eight hours of sunlight—or partial sun for some shade plants
- a water source nearby
- adequate soil drainage

A suitable garden plot is defined only by the amount of your landscape you wish to dedicate that possesses all three of these desirable attributes. This includes the amount of space in your home you wish to allot to container gardening.

If you have a small space or poor soil conditions, raised beds, container gardening, and square-foot gardening are all viable methods for raising healthy fruits and vegetables. Each method has advantages and disadvantages. Gardeners often choose a combination of methods if a larger backyard space is available.

Raised Beds	Container	Square Foot
A framed soil bed raised off the ground	Transportable container used for planting	Square raised bed. Garden is divided into a grid of square-foot sections
Soil drains well	Drainage system needed (holes in the planter, rocks)	Soil drains well
Good root growth potential	Container size will dictate root growth potential	Good root growth potential
Less weeding needed than traditional garden	Relatively little weeding needed	Less weeding needed than traditional garden
Less watering needed	Frequent watering needed	Less watering needed

Good for areas with poor soil, rock and slopes	Good for any area, allows gardening in small spaces that may otherwise be inaccessible	Good for areas with poor soil, rock and slopes
Large amount of soil needed	Soil needs are dictated by container size	Large amount of soil needed
Extra materials required to construct bed	Containers required to plant	May or may not need extra materials to construct bed
Large area for planting	Planting area dictated by container size	Large area for planting
Seeds can be planted in rows	Seed planting dictated by size and shape of container	Conservative use of seeds, designed for succession gardening
Easy to protect from insects and predators	Easy to protect from insects and predators	Easy to protect from insects and predators

THE LITTLE CONTAINER THAT COULD

Do you have a small backyard or apartment? Container gardening is the perfect solution for enjoying fresh fruits and vegetables throughout the year. It's a great tool and a truly versatile solution for any gardener or plant lover. Even though I have a rather large garden, I still container-garden herbs and other plants to keep them close for cooking, and also to brighten up the house with fresh greenery.

Space-intensive plants, such as corn, pumpkins, and melons, are not the best container garden candidates, but there are plenty of options available, some that may surprise you, like coffee, peanuts, bananas, and quinoa.

Ideal Plants for Container Gardening				
Aloe Vera	Apple Trees	Avocados	Bananas	Blackberries
Blueberries	Carrots	Cherries	Citrus Fruits	Cucumbers
Figs	Green Beans	Herbs (all)	Hops	Lettuce (all varieties)
Mushrooms	Peas	Peppers	Potatoes	Quinoa
Squash	Strawberries	Tomatoes		

The primary concern with container plants is water. If the plants are in the house or on sheltered areas like patios, they may need daily watering. Outdoor plants may also need to be brought inside during storms, which will further reduce the amount of water they need to survive. If the soil feels dry to the touch, add water until they're hydrated (but not soggy).

 Chick Tip: Collect rain water for your container garden. Place small buckets outside on a patio or at the end of gutter systems, then bring it inside to give your plants a dose of what nature provides.

A secondary concern may be pollination. Plants like tomatoes and cucumbers need to be pollinated. Indoors, there are no bees, animals, or breezes to help pollinate your plants. If you are able to set the plant outside, maybe on a balcony, this will often solve your pollination dilemma. If not, there are three tools you can use to help the plant to pollinate:

1. Tabletop Fan—Use a standard indoor fan to create a simulated breeze to help move the pollen around.

2. Electric Toothbrush—Use an inexpensive vibrating electric toothbrush to gently shake the plant to encourage the spread of pollen. Each day, simply place the toothbrush on the stem of the plant for a few seconds and then near each individual flower.

3. Cotton Swab—Plants that have male and female flowers, like cucumbers, need to have pollen moved from the male flower to the female. Use a cotton swab to collect pollen from the male flower and then spread it inside the female flower. *Note:* Male flowers will have a visible powdery substance (pollen) inside them and female flowers will not. The female flower will usually be slightly larger and contain the beginning bud of vegetable or fruit.

Additional conditions needed for container gardening are a warm location, such as a sunroom, balcony, or screened porch, and an area with adequate sunlight, such as a south-facing window. If an adequate light source is not available, grow lights will be a good investment.

Container gardens are not only friendly for small spaces, they are terrific for coaxing year-round produce through succession planting. As soon as you harvest a crop from your container, remove plant materials, add soil if needed, and plant a new series of seeds.

Ideal choices for containers are those made of wood, clay, metal or plastic. Drainage holes are often suggested as a necessity, but I find they can be a hassle when the plants are residing indoors. In this case, I prefer to use a thin layer of racks to create a drainage space at the bottom of the container.

Size, on the other hand, does matter. The container must be an appropriate size to allow the plant to grow. Carrots will not thrive in shallow plant pots, and a five-gallon bucket will be wasted space if you are planting herbs like mint or parsley, which do not require deep root space.

Think vertical for vine crops such as cucumbers, pole beans, and tomatoes. Hanging baskets, trellises, cages, and fences all work well with these types of plants.

Explore optional alternatives for container gardening, such as recycling used items like ceramic cups and bowls and new methods of growing plants, such as aquaponics. Aquaponic containers grow plants without soil, merging fish tanks with planters, creating a symbiotic relationship between the two life forms.

HOW TO RECORD WHAT YOU SOW

Prior to starting your garden, or just as you begin planting, begin keeping a garden journal. This guide will become an invaluable resource, offering insights, history, and handy reminders. A simple spiral notebook will suffice, or a basic software spreadsheet. Custom journal programs are available through online resources and plenty of apps are beginning to surface too. Use whatever resource suits your style. An iPad can be carried to the garden just as easily as a notepad.

Handy information to track in your journal is:

- Date of the last frost in your region
- Date of the first frost in your region
- Types of seeds you are planting
- Dates you purchased seeds
- Dates you planted seeds
- Dates you harvested produce
- Amount of produce harvested per plant
- Dates you harvested seeds
- Amount of seeds harvested
- Date seeds were stored
- Daily or weekly observations
- Notes on successes and mishaps
- Lessons learned in the garden
- Soil test dates and results
- Rainfall dates and amounts
- Fertilizers and natural remedies used
- Date fertilizers and natural remedies were used
- Thoughts and ideas you have for current and future needs

When you are finished gardening for the year, tuck the journal away, then pull it out before the next planting season as a guide.

SOW, SOW, SOW YOUR SEEDS!

The basic steps for planting seeds are easy to follow:
- Soil should be moist
- Seeds should be aligned in straight rows (check package for proper spacing)
- Plant seeds at proper depth (check package for proper depth)
- Sow seeds in larger quantities than needed to help ensure germination
- Cover seeds and firm soil by patting down gently with the side of a hoe blade
- Keep rows moistened after planting; dry seeds will not germinate

When seeds begin sprouting, you may need to thin out the plants and, when possible, transplant the thinnings. Plants that do not need to be thinned until harvest include lettuce, onions, and radishes.

While most seeds will do well when sown directly, some varieties, like bell peppers, broccoli, cabbage, eggplant, and tomatoes, are better as transplants. Transplants are started indoors and later transplanted into your outdoor garden.

Seed starting kits are available for purchase, or you can make your own by using ordinary items such as egg cartons, yogurt containers, or soup cans. A clear plastic dome, bag, or sheet will suffice to lock in humidity while allowing sunlight in. Starter soil can be purchased at any nursery or farm store, or you can put your own simple mix together with a 1:1 ratio of sphagnum peat moss and vermiculite.

 Chick Tip: Use eggshells to plant your starter seeds. After cracking eggs open for cooking, gently rinse residue from the eggshell halves. Fill an eggshell half with starter soil and plant a seed as normal. When it's ready for transplant, remove the plant from the eggshell, and then compost the eggshell to help fertilize the plant later.

Starter seeds need sunshine and water. Each variety has its own germination period, typically around two months (check your seed packet for germination information). Ideally, you should start your seeds at the time recommended prior to your last expected, or average, frost date. To find out about frost dates in your area, contact your local County Cooperative Extension Office, check weather channel information, or consult the *Farmer's Almanac* guide for your area.

When plants are ready for transplant, an adjustment period called hardening is needed. Seven to ten days prior to the desired planting time, set containers outside in a semi-shaded area with indirect sunlight, such as a patio or screened porch, for two hours the first day. Increase time outdoors by two hours per day for one week. If a cold spell is expected, though, be sure to bring the plants inside, regardless of whether they have been out for the prescribed length of time.

When the plant is sufficiently hardened and ready to transplant, plant a sampling of two to four plants in the garden and monitor them for two days. If the plants thrive well, transplant the entire set.

There are many opinions about the best time to transplant. I have found early morning, about an hour after sunrise, to be ideal.

 Chick Tip: Create labels for your starter seeds using wooden sticks (like recycled Popsicle sticks) and a permanent marker to record the name of the plant and date of planting. Even with the best of intentions, if starter plants are not marked, it's easy to forget what seeds you have started when and where!

THE ELEMENT OF WATER

Under optimum conditions, outdoor gardens will receive adequate moisture from nature. However, as every gardener knows, Mother Nature is not always as cooperative as we may prefer.

Vegetables and fruits require approximately one inch of water per week. A rain gauge can help keep you from guessing whether the afternoon sun shower delivered enough water to nourish your plants.

Garden hoses, sprinklers, trickle irrigation, and overhead irrigation systems are all adequate alternative water delivery systems to use when enough rainfall is not delivered.

One of my favorite eco-friendly options is to use rain barrels in conjunction with a water hose. Using a standard gutter drainage system, the water is funneled to rain barrels. You can use water you collect in times of drought. You can purchase retail versions or find DIY plans through various sources, including your local conservation offices. Fifty-five-gallon food-grade plastic drums make excellent rain barrels. Check with your local farmers or on craigslist.com to find offerings near you.

Water in the morning to give plants time to dry off before nightfall. Moisture left on foliage can lead to issues with diseases and rot. Do not over-water plants either; over-watering is a plant disease-spreading magnet.

WELCOME TO THE JUNGLE

An average outdoor garden contains thousands of insects and a wide variety of weeds. Most gardeners aren't very happy to see either pest, but they are all part of the delicate balance of nature and, surprisingly, some are beneficial to your gardening efforts.

Four basic gardening principles must be in place to help prevent insect infestations and wild weeds from overrunning your efforts. Essentially, you must WHIP (Weed, sHift, Interplant, Plow) your garden into shape!

Weed

Weeds and bugs go hand in hand, so, to help control both simultaneously, weed often. Remove the roots of the weed whenever possible to prevent regrowth.

Plants also need adequate space for good air circulation. Weeds can crowd the garden and cause air circulation to be poor, creating ideal situations for fungus and other diseases to flourish.

Weed seeds can remain dormant in soil for years. Pull weeds early before they reach the seed stage to help prevent regrowth.

Shift

A general rule of green thumb is to shift or rotate crops every one to two years and avoid planting closely related crops in the same spots. For example, rotating cabbage to the spot where you just had kale will not be effective. These plants are plagued by the same insects and diseases.

Rotating crops regularly helps the soil to recover, and it is also confusing for bugs. Many bugs lie dormant in the ground waiting for a new crop. When a crop they aren't keen on pops up instead of last year's offering, it may keep the bugs from reinfesting.

Interplant

Interplanting, or companion planting, involves planting two complementary crops such as corn and cucumbers in the same garden space or adjoining spaces. The cucumbers help regulate weeds naturally for corn, and corn provides shade and climbing poles for the cucumbers.

On the other side of the coin, plants like cabbage and kale are better off on polar opposite sides of the garden. They share common bugs, and there's no need to up the temptation factor for full-blown infestations.

Plants like marigolds, onions, and garlic are known to be helpful in repelling bugs and may be interspersed throughout crops, though onions and garlic do not mix well with plants like asparagus. Refer to the chart on pages 66 and 67 for common companions.

Plow

New soil should be turned over in the spring at a depth of eight to ten inches for a fresh plot. Old soil should be turned under in the fall to help decomposition. Both these practices help keep the soil in tip-top shape and expose insect larvae and pupae to the elements, which often causes them to die.

When you are turning soil in the fall, let it serve as a reminder to have your soil tested. Your local County Extension Office or a private lab-testing facility will be able to guide you in collecting a sample and analyzing the results.

 Chick Tip: Want sweeter tomato plants? Sprinkle baking soda around the base of the tomato plant once per week (prior to watering). The baking soda lowers the acidity in the soil, which translates into plump, sweet tomatoes on the vine.

Quick Guide to Companion Plants	
PLANT	**PREFERRED COMPANION PLANTS**
Asparagus	Carrots, dill, parsley, tomatoes
Basil	Asparagus, bell peppers, oregano, tomatoes
Bay Leaves	Cayenne peppers, peppermint
Beets	Cabbage, lettuce, garlic, onions
Bell Peppers	Basil, carrots, geraniums, marigolds, onions, parsley
Broccoli	Cucumbers, dill, garlic, lettuce, onions, rhubarb, rosemary, sage, thyme
Cabbage	Beets, celery, chamomile, dill, mustard, onions, potatoes, rhubarb, sage
Carrots	Asparagus, chives, lettuce, onions
Celery	Cabbage, daisies, green beans, tomatoes
Chives	Apple trees, carrots, tomatoes
Cilantro	Anise, dill, potatoes
Corn	Cantaloupe, cucumbers, green beans, morning glories, parsley, peas, pumpkins, squash, sunflowers, watermelon
Cucumbers	Carrots, corn, garlic, green beans, marigolds, peas, radishes, sunflower
Eggplant	Green beans, okra, peas, spinach, thyme, marigolds
Garlic	Apple trees, cucumbers, lettuce, peach trees, pear trees, peas, raspberries
Grapes	Basil, blackberries, geraniums, oregano, peas
Green Beans	Carrots, celery, corn, cucumbers, eggplant, potatoes, radishes, strawberries

Horseradish	Potatoes
Lavender	Fruit Trees
Lettuce	Beets, broccoli, carrots, cucumbers, dill, marigolds, okra, onions, radishes, strawberries
Onions	Beets, carrots, chamomile, dill, lettuce, radishes, strawberries, tomatoes
Oregano	Broccoli, cabbage, cauliflower
Peas	Bell peppers, carrots, corn, celery, cucumbers, eggplant, parsley, radishes, spinach, tomatoes
Potatoes	Cabbage, carrots, celery, corn, flax, green beans, horseradish, marigolds, peas, onions, squash
Pumpkins	Corn, cantaloupe, marigolds, musk melon, squash, watermelon
Radishes	Carrots, cucumbers, lettuce, green beans, marigolds, mustard, onions, spinach, squash, watermelon
Rosemary	Cabbage, carrots, green beans, sage
Sage	Broccoli, cabbage, cauliflower, rosemary
Spinach	Cabbage, cauliflower, celery, green beans, eggplant, lima beans, onions, peas, strawberries
Squash	Corn, cucumbers, dill, green beans, marigolds, mint, onions, oregano, pumpkins, radishes
Sweet Potatoes	Beets, dill, oregano, rosemary, thyme
Strawberries	Green beans, lettuce, marigolds, onions, spinach, thyme
Tomatoes	Asparagus, basil, bell peppers, celery, chives, cucumbers, garlic, green beans, marigolds, mint, onions, parsley, peas
Watermelon	Corn, marigolds, nasturtiums, pumpkins, radishes, squash, sunflowers

I've whipped the garden into shape, but I'm still having insect problems. What now?

I'm personally not anti-insect. All insects are beneficial to our ecosystem, but some may be exceptionally harmful to plants, taking over and destroying your garden. To maintain a healthy garden, insect control is a necessity.

Pesticides may be applied, but before you pull out the poisons, consider the many organic methods for removing bugs from plants that will not release harmful chemicals into the environment or taint your food supply. The next time you have a bug problem in your garden, try one of these tried-and-true methods:

- Pick bugs by hand: squash them individually, then drop them in a bucket to feed to your chickens or compost.
- Check plant leaves and scrape off any eggs into a bucket to feed to your chickens or to dispose of by burning.
- Use floating row covers in your garden to discourage bugs from invading plants.
- Use netting for fruit bushes to help keep fruit flies and other insects off plants.
- Spray water regularly and forcefully on hardy plants. This is especially helpful in controlling aphids.
- Use insecticidal soap on plants per manufacturer directions.
- Use a mix of one cup of flour to three cups of water to spray on plants. When it dries, this mixture stops grubs and caterpillars in their tracks.
- Use a mix of equal parts buttermilk and water to spray on leaves of plants.
- Brew cedar chips in warm water, then spray on plants. This is particularly helpful with squash bugs.
- Use diatomaceous earth to rid plants of ants, aphids, and maggots.
- Use Tanglefoot around base of trees to help protect against climbing insects.
- Place collars around stems of transplants to prevent worm damage.
- Wrap aluminum foil around the base of tree trunks to help keep borers from climbing the trunk.

- Try planting earlier or later in the season to avoid prime insect feeding times during the summer months.
- Use black plastic ground covers to help keep maggots from traveling through the soil. The cover also serves as a weed barrier and moisture retainer for soil.
- Choose resistant seed varieties for common pest problems in your area.

WHY IS MY PLANT SICK?

There are four basic types of disease classifications: fungi, bacteria, nematodes, and viruses. Diseases are typically carried to plants by insects, people, or birds, or caused by poor nutrition and environmental stressors. Seeds may also carry viruses, or wind may carry diseases over from another garden. Often the cause cannot be determined. The most important thing to remember is to treat the disease as soon as you spot it to keep it from spreading to other plants.

Nonchemical methods can be highly effective in the treatment of diseases. Following the WHIP plan (see pages 64 and 65) will also help prevent and rid your garden of diseases. Plants, though, like people, can fall prey to diseases despite your best efforts. Use the chart on pages 70 through 72 to help you identify and treat some of the most common plant diseases.

There are thousands of diseases. If you do not find one on the chart, or if your plant is exhibiting systems that are not listed, consult your local conservation office or county extension office to help identify and treat the disease your plant is experiencing.

Common Diseases and Treatments			
DISEASE	**AFFECTS**	**SYMPTOMS**	**CURE**
Allium Smut	Garlic, onions	Black spots on leaves and bulbs	Destroy infected plants. Rotate crops during next growing season.
Anthrac-nose	Peppers	Sunken dark spots on fruit	Improve weed control. Remove affected plants at the end of the growing season.
Bacterial Blight	Beans	Large brown spots on leaves and beans	Avoid handling beans in moist conditions. Pull all vines and burn at the end of the growing season. Rotate crops during next growing season.
Bacterial Spotting	Tomatoes, peppers	Small, brown, circular spots on leaves and fruit	Remove affected plants. Rotate crops during next growing season.
Black Rot	Broccoli, Brussels sprouts, cabbage, cauliflower	Black veins on plant and yellowing leaves	Provide good soil drainage and air circulation around plants. Rotate crops during next growing season.

Corn Smut	Corn	Stalk and ears develop large galls, which later blacken	Pick galls off plants and burn. Destroy and burn plants after growing season. Rotate crops during next growing season.
Early Blight	Tomatoes, potatoes	Dark brown spots on leaves, stem, or fruit; decay of plant or fruit	Remove affected areas.
Fusarium Wilt	Celery	Stalks and leaves develop red tissue, yellowing leaves	Improve soil health. Rotate crops for several growing seasons.
Late Blight	Tomatoes, potatoes, carrots	Dark brown spots on leaves, stem, or fruit; decay of plant or fruit White or yellow spots on leaves, lesions on roots	Remove affected areas
Mosaic	Cucumbers, pumpkins, squash	Fruit whitens or yellows, and leaves take on a rough, blotchy appearance	Check nearby weeds for signs of disease; pull and burn weeds and affected plants.
Phomopsis Blight	Eggplant	Small, light brown spots will quickly grow and spread	Remove affected plants at the end of the growing season.

Powdery Mildew	Tomatoes	Yellow spots on leaves, followed by leaf death	Remove affected plants at the end of the growing season. Improve air circulation to prevent spreading or reoccurrence.
Rust	Asparagus, lettuce (all varieties), beans, spinach, carrots, eggplant	Reddish-yellow spots on plant, leading to plant death	Space plants widely to ensure better air circulation. Remove affected plants after harvest season and burn.

To further help prevent diseases or the spread of diseases in your garden, always wash your hands and tools before working in your garden and especially after handling diseased plants. Use certified disease-free seeds for planting, and be sure to always offer plants a growing area with good soil drainage and good air circulation.

THINKING OF FRUITS? START WITH NATURE'S FIRST LOVE

Strawberries have long been associated with all things amore. From adorning Valentine's Day tables in chocolate-dipped coats to posing as the symbol for Venus, goddess of love, this succulent, heart-shaped beauty is a treat to eat and grow. It also happens to be a gardener's best fruit friend, whether you have a green thumb or not, flourishing in small beds and container gardens as well as in wide open spaces.

The three biggest challenges you'll have in growing strawberries are:
1. Keeping the weeds at bay
2. Keeping the plants from taking over your garden
3. Trying not to eat all the strawberries before you can get them from garden to table!

Like most other plants, strawberries need a well-drained soil bed. Unlike some other hardy produce, strawberries will die if they get too wet, so good soil drainage is absolutely essential.

Two main types of strawberry plants are everbearing and June-bearing. Everbearing will typically produce a small crop in the spring, large crops throughout the summer, and another small crop in the fall. June-bearing, as their name indicates, will produce one large crop during the summer (which, depending upon what planting zone you live in, may or may not be in June).

If you are container gardening, everbearing is the best choice, as you'll maximize your efforts with a longer production period.

The best time to plant strawberries in most zones is early spring. Initially, very few strawberry plants are needed, as each plant will produce runners that will quickly root and produce new offspring. In fact, an excellent way to begin strawberry gardening is to borrow a runner or two from your neighbors. Ask them to train a few runners from their healthiest plants into a small planter for you to use, and you'll soon be on your way to enjoying fresh strawberries.

A challenge with strawberry plant runners is controlling them. If you get too many, the strawberry plants will soon take over whatever space you'll allotted them, as well as every other growing space they can find nearby. Overcrowded strawberry plants will not produce well, and, unless all you ever want to harvest from your garden are strawberries, you'll need a plan of attack to control the runners.

Shooting an arrow in the runners of love

Strawberry plant runners are the long stems that grow off the central plant. Each runner produces new baby strawberry plants. Runners rob the central plant of nutrients and will cause the central plant to produce less fruit. For this reason, all runners should be pinched off brand-new strawberry plants in the first season to allow the central plant to flourish.

After the first season of crops, new runners can:
- be allowed to grow and expand your strawberry garden, thinned out as necessary
- be allowed to grow and then later weeded out, chopped, and fed to your chickens or composted
- be trained to grow into small plant containers (filled with soil), then given to a friend or neighbor who wishes to grow strawberries or transplanted to a new container, bed, or area of your garden.

Removing a runner is quite simple. Follow the runner stem to the central plant and pinch it off about a half-inch from the central plant.

Nurturing and nourishing your little red sweethearts

Strawberries need plenty of water and lots of weed control. Hand weeding is the best method and should be done daily, especially during early plant growth, to keep the weeds under control. Weeds rob strawberry plants of vital nutrients and water; controlling them will help your strawberries thrive.

Birds, including chickens, are another set of natural enemies to your strawberry patch. If you'd like to enjoy your strawberries, you must keep the birds out with fencing or netting.

Insects and disease are lesser concerns but still potential problems. Keeping your strawberry patch well-weeded will help you avoid both troubles. Slugs are the biggest pest invaders of strawberry plants, due to mulching. You can hand-pick the slugs off and relocate them. Or try an old home remedy: bury a small, flat bowl or container, such as a pie pan, in the center of your strawberry bed so that the lip of the container is even with the soil. Fill the container with beer, leave it for a night or two, and presto! Slugs will no longer be an issue.

Mulching (or covering) strawberries to protect them from cold weather is a necessity. Wheat or rye straw is one of the most effective materials you can use to cover the strawberry plants. Unfortunately, these are also the materials that attract the aforementioned slugs. Place a layer of three-to-five-inches of straw over your strawberry patch when the weather consistently drops below 40 degrees. Remove the mulch in the spring when the threat of frost has passed.

If you are container gardening, don't leave containers housing strawberries outside in dormant months. Even if you add a layer of mulch, small containers are typically no match for frigid temperatures. Apply a layer of mulch to the tops of the containers and store them in a barn or shed area that is well sheltered from the wind and elements. If the containers reside predominantly inside, remove the container from light sources and cover it with a thin layer of shredded newspaper. This will encourage the plant to remain in dormancy until spring. Strawberry plants that are dormant in the winter months will produce better throughout the spring and summer.

Harvest strawberries when the fruit is fully ripened. When picking strawberries, pick the caps along with the fruit, and be careful not to squish or bruise the fruit. The caps may be cut off prior to storage, but should ideally be kept on until you are ready to use, consume, or freeze the berries. Save the caps to compost or feed to chickens.

Strawberries will keep up to a week in the refrigerator. Do not wash strawberries prior to storing in the refrigerator; water will quickly turn them to mush and accelerate rotting of the fruit. Though strawberries from the farmers market come in crates, the best way to store strawberries in a refrigerator is in a single layer. Line a pan or storage container with towels or paper towels, and arrange the strawberries in a single layer. This will dramatically increase your chances of keeping the strawberries fresh for a week or slightly longer.

SARAH'S STRAWBERRY PRETZEL DELIGHT

Our family devours gobs of fresh strawberries in the summer months. Very few ever make it to the freezer or to jam stage. I made relatively few desserts with strawberries, though, until my husband reminisced about a strawberry dessert that his mother, Sarah, used to make when he was growing up. I was able to obtain a copy of the recipe, and we've enjoyed it ever since. I serve it on occasion as a special treat or for picnics and parties. There's hardly a leftover crumb to spare! When it comes to the fruit of love, there's no other recipe I could substitute that holds so much endearment and rich summer flavor.

Ingredients:

2 cups pretzels

½ cup butter

1 cup sugar

4 cups whipped cream

2 cups cream cheese

2 cups hot water

1 16-ounce package of
  strawberry gelatin

2 cups fresh strawberries,
  capped and
  sliced

Preheat oven to 400 degrees Fahrenheit.

On a clean, flat surface use a rolling pin to crush pretzels and set them aside. In a small saucepan over medium heat, add butter. Cook until melted, remove from heat, and cool for 10 minutes. Mix crushed pretzels into cooled butter. Spread an even layer of the pretzel-butter mixture over the bottom of a 9 x 13-inch pan.

Bake pretzel layer for 10 minutes. Remove from oven, set pan on baking rack, and cool until pretzel crust is room temperature (or cool to your touch).

In a large mixing bowl, add sugar, whipped cream and cream cheese. Whip until fully blended. Spread cream cheese mix evenly over cooled pretzel crust. Seal the edges of the cream cheese layer by running a spoon along the seam of the pan. It's important to completely seal the cream cheese layer over the pretzel crust, or you will later wind up with a soggy crust. Set baking pan aside to cool in refrigerator.

In a medium mixing bowl, add hot water to strawberry gelatin. Stir until gelatin is fully dissolved. Allow gelatin to cool until partially set. Add sliced strawberries to the partially set gelatin, and stir gently to coat berries with gelatin.

Remove baking dish with pretzel and cream cheese layers from refrigerator. Pour gelatin and strawberry mix evenly over cream cheese layer. Refrigerate baking dish until gelatin is completely set and the dessert is ready to serve. Cut into squares, plate, and serve. Optionally, garnish plates with additional strawberry slices.

HARNESS THE POWER OF THE PAST

The case for seed saving has never been stronger. Right now there are around 10,000 plant varieties at risk of endangerment or extinction. In addition to providing plant biodiversity for the earth, many of these seeds are edible varieties that provide immense flavor and nutrients when cultivated. Edible seeds include alfalfa (sprouts), chia (sprouts), flax, poppy, pumpkin, and sunflower.

Our fragile ecosystems are dependent upon seed savers. As climate changes continue, the need for seeds that will thrive in variant regions is paramount. By saving seeds you're not only saving yourself money and potentially adding diversity to your diet, you are helping to protect our culture, heritage, legacy, and planet.

If you plan to seed-save, you must begin with untreated heirloom seeds. They may be obtained from various retail mail companies, farm store locations, and seed banks like the Seed Savers Exchange (seedsavers.org).

Only a few plants need to be grown for seed harvesting. There's no need to harvest a large crop of seeds unless you plan to use some for sprouting, to share with friends, or to expand your produce production the following year.

Many seeds can be harvested by gently shaking the dried plant or by threshing, a method in which dry plants are hit against the side of a container, causing the seeds to fall out. Plants may vary in the manner in which seeds can be collected. Consult with your local extension agency, a seed bank, university agriculture department, or farm agency to help determine the best methods.

Herb seeds are among the easiest to collect. Many herb seeds—like celery, dill, mustard and anise—are terrific for seasoning dishes and baked goods. To collect herb seeds, pick plants when the seed pods are fully formed but not dried (the plant may still be green). Dry plant stalks and pods indoors on mesh racks. Place a clean, dry cloth under the rack to catch the seeds. Collect dried seeds and store in an airtight container in a cool, dry, dark spot like the pantry or a cupboard to use for seasoning or for planting in the next growing season.

At the beginning of the next planting cycle, you may test the viability of your seeds easily with a wet paper towel. Simply scatter about a dozen seeds on the towel, then fold it over with the seeds to the inside. Fold it a second time to form a square and place it inside a self-sealing plastic bag. Seal the bag and place it on a windowsill that receives full sunlight during the day.

In two weeks, open the bag and unfold the paper towel. If more than half the seeds have sprouted, you have a good seed batch.

DIY: SPROUT YOUR OWN SEEDS

Sprouting is a popular practice and a fun, tasty way to grow fresh vegetables in the winter and add nutrients to your diet. Sprouts are frequently used in salads, breads, sandwiches and soups. Though they can be cooked, the best way to enjoy sprouts to take advantage of their flavor and nutrients is to eat them raw.

Common seeds for sprouting are soy, radish, fava beans, lima beans, garbanzo beans, pinto beans, mustard, chia, peas, flax, and lentils. Some gardeners also enjoy sprouting seeds like sunflower, pumpkin, and lettuce seeds. Sprouting oatmeal for your chickens is a fabulous and beneficial winter treat too (see recipe below).

Here are three very important things to remember when you're selecting seeds for sprouting:

- Seeds that should not be used for sprouting include potato, tomato, sorghum, and fruit seeds. These seeds are considered to be toxic.
- Garden seeds, especially treated varieties, are not suitable for sprouting and may contain toxic elements.
- Use only untreated heirloom seeds saved from your garden, or purchase seeds specifically intended for sprouting. Many seed stores and whole-food stores carry sprouting seeds.

Various methods and materials exist for sprouting seeds, ranging from earthenware sprouters to wooden sprouting boxes. The simplest method, and the best one to begin with to determine if enjoying sprouts is something you wish to do regularly, is the Mason jar method (see recipes on pages 80 and 81).

Sprouts are very low-maintenance plants. They don't require any soil or sunlight (though some sprouts taste better with sun sprouting). All that most sprouts really need is a constant warm room temperature (65–75 degrees Fahrenheit) and regular intervals of wetting with water.

MASON JAR METHOD: PINTO BEAN SPROUTS

Ingredients:

½ cup pinto beans

Warm water

1-quart Mason jar, wide-mouth
style

1 Mason jar ring, wide-mouth
style

6-inch square of cheesecloth

Soak pinto beans in a cup of warm water for one minute, then rinse. Pour seeds into Mason jar. Add 2 cups of warm water. Cover the jar with cheesecloth and use Mason jar ring to secure. Set in a cool, dry, dark place for 8–12 hours.

Drain water completely from jar through cheesecloth. Lay jar on its side. Gently move back and forth and side to side to distribute seeds along one side of the jar. Set the jar in a sunny, dry space for 12 hours.

Uncap jar, rinse seeds with 2 cups of warm water. Recap jar with cheesecloth. Drain water completely through cheesecloth. Lay jar on side and rescatter sprouts along one side of the jar. Set jar in a sunny, dry space for 12 hours. Continue to repeat process every 12 hours until the sprouts are about 1 inch long. (The process will take about 6–8 days.)

When sprouts reach desired length, they are ready to eat. Remove them from the jar, wash in cool water, and remove seed covers (if preferred). Drain completely. If there are any roots visible, simply snip them before eating.

 Chick Tip: Extra sprouts may be stored in the refrigerator for up to a week. If you have an abundance of sprouts, try drying and crumbling them to use later as seasoning for soups and stews.

MASON JAR METHOD: OATMEAL SPROUTS

Ingredients:
½ cup hulled oats
1-quart Mason jar, wide-mouth style
1 Mason jar ring, wide-mouth style
6-inch square of cheesecloth
Warm water

Rinse oats in warm water and pour into a Mason jar. Add 2 cups of warm water. Cover the jar with cheesecloth and use Mason jar ring to secure. Set jar to the side in cool, dry, dark place for 6–8 hours. Oats should double in size.

Rinse oats, drain water completely from jar through cheesecloth. Lay jar on its side. Gently move back and forth and roll jar to distribute seeds along sides of the jar. Set in a sunny, dry space for 8 hours.

Uncap jar, rinse seeds with 2 cups of warm water. Recap jar with cheesecloth. Drain water completely through cheesecloth. Lay jar on side and rescatter sprouts around the jar. Set in a sunny, dry space for 8 hours. Continue to repeat process every 8 hours until the sprouts are the same length as the length of the oat seed. (The process will take about 2–3 days.)

When sprouts reach desired length, they are ready to eat. Remove the sprouts from the jar, wash in cool water, and remove seed covers (if preferred). Drain completely.

Oatmeal sprouts may also be enjoyed in your morning breakfast bowl or used in baking, but the joy of seeing your chickens' delight when they are fed this fresh treat is plenty rewarding!

 Chick Tip: Oats are also an excellent cover crop for your outdoor garden. Sow oat seeds through the entire garden area to help improve soil, prevent soil erosion, and control weeds.

REPLENISHING MOTHER EARTH

The world is an ecosystem, particularly the plant world. Plants spring from the earth to provide nourishment, then offer nourishment to the earth and new plant growth when they decompose. This sustainable cycle of recycling nutrients back into the soil creates nutrient- and mineral-rich soil.

Basically, to compost means to create organic matter through the natural decomposing of plant material or animal waste products of herbivores. If done regularly, composting eliminates the need for chemical fertilizers, nourishes plants, and promotes growth. In the average home around one-quarter to one-half of all household waste can be composted.

Methods of composting include:

Worm composting (vermicomposting)—A worm farm is set up in the kitchen, on a balcony, or in a bigger box located outside the home. Worms are highly beneficial to the compost process and will speed up the composting. If you have an outdoor compost pile, there's no need to add worms to it; the worms will find it. If you have an indoor compost bin, you will need to add the worms.

Chicken composting—Simply feed your chickens weeds and scraps, then use chicken droppings to compost.

Garden composting—Wet and dry layers are alternated in a pile at the edge of the garden away from any plant growth: first a layer of dried grass clippings, then a layer of shredded newspaper, and so on. Mix once a week with a pitchfork or rake.

Another version is sheet composting. Dig a one-foot-deep trench. Add vegetable scraps, plant materials, and other compost materials. Cover with a layer of soil. Leave to compost over the course of the year.

Bin composting—An interior or exterior bin is set up to collect compost scraps. There are a slew of modern choices available, including countertop and under-the-counter options to help you with your composting efforts.

Community composting—A neighborhood compost spot is established as a community garden compost location. Be sure to check with your city or town; you may already have an established city compost initiative in place.

Donation composting—When you do not have an area of your own to compost, collect scraps and work with a neighbor or nearby farmer to contribute to their composting efforts.

City composting—Bins are designated for pickup by city recycling or sanitation services. If your city does not participate, contact local officials and plant the idea!

Common materials to compost

There are plenty of everyday items that are easily composted. Some are easy to identify, such as weeds or citrus peels. Others may surprise you, like cotton balls and dryer lint.

All the materials listed in this chart are everyday items that can and *should* be composted regularly:

Chicken feathers	Potato peelings
Fruits	Corn stalks
Popcorn	Hay
Citrus peelings	Printer paper
Grass clippings	Corrugated cardboard (uncoated)
Potato chips	Household dust
Coffee grounds	Pulp from juicing
Haircut clippings	Cotton balls

Human hair

Sawdust

Cotton fabrics (100%)

Newspaper

Seaweed

Cotton swabs (with paper barrel)

Nutshells

Spices

Cover crops

Paper bags

Straw

Dryer lint

Paper coffee filters

Tea bags

Eggshells

Paper or wood matches

Tofu

Facial tissues

Paper plates, cups and napkins

Twigs

Fall leaves

Pasta

Vegetables

Flowers

Pet hair

Weeds

Freezer-burnt fruit

Pine needles

Wooden toothpicks

Freezer-burnt vegetables

Plants

Writing paper

Manure from herbivores such as rabbits, mice, horses, cows, and chickens may be composted as well. Cool manure—from rabbits, cattle, horses, and sheep—may be used regularly in compost piles and may also be regularly applied directly to soil as a fertilizer. Hot manure—from pigs, chickens, ducks, and other fowl—may also be composted regularly but should be used sparingly in direct application as a plant fertilizer as they are rich in nitrogen and may burn plants.

Common materials that SHOULD NOT be composted

Baked goods	Dairy products
Household cleaners	Meat by-products (fat, bone)
Charcoal ashes	Diapers
Human or carnivorous animal waste	Oils
Coated cardboard	Diseased plants
Insect-infested plants	Pizza boxes
Coated papers	Grease
Meat	Treated wood

There are different philosophies about what may and may not be composted. For example, some people do choose to compost dairy products or baked goods. If you have an outdoor compost, the best practice is not to compost these items, as they attract animals and other pests, turning your compost pile into a feeding frenzy. If you are composting in a different manner—for example, using your chickens as your primary compost method—they may love most of the dairy and grain products you toss in the coop.

DIY: MAKE YOUR OWN INDOOR VERMICOMPOSTER

Worms are earth's natural soil-dwelling composters. When the worm is finished digesting organic matter, it releases nutrient-rich compost.

To make your own vermicomposter, you will need:
- A 5- to 10-gallon rectangular container
- A wooden box lined with plastic, a plastic tub, or an old aquarium (all great choices for this project)
- A loose-fitting cover for your container
- Moist newspaper strips
- Red wigglers or red worms.

In the case of indoor vermicomposting, all worms are not created equal. You will not be able to simply dig up night crawlers from your front yard; you must have red worms that thrive on organic matter. Purchase red worms or red wigglers from local worm farms or via mail order. Keep in mind that worms breed quickly, doubling their population about every three months, so don't be tempted to over-purchase. For every square foot of surface in your worm bin, you will need about 1,000 worms.

In addition to supplies, and perhaps more importantly, you need to have the correct environment for your worms to be happy and productive. Worms must have:

- Moisture
- Good air circulation
- A dark location
- Warm temperatures (but not too hot—worm bins should not be placed next to a direct source of heat like a radiator)

Once you have your environment picked out and your materials gathered, it's time to start building your vermicompost bin.

First, fill your container about halfway with layers of moist newspaper strips. Do not fill the container to the top; worms like to dwell in about the top six inches of soil, so if you fill it too high they will rarely get down to the bottom of the bin.

Next, add your worms, cover the container lightly (never completely seal the container as it will cut off the much-needed air supply), and store the container in a dark, warm location.

Begin feeding your worms slowly. Initially they will begin to feast on the newspaper strips, but will soon be in need of organic matter to digest. Add compost scraps, in small quantities at first, in a thin layer across the top of the newspaper. Once the bin is established and you notice the scraps disappearing, add more compost materials.

Worms enjoy feasting on vegetables, fruit, pasta, bread, wet paper, crushed eggshells, coffee grounds, tea bags (for best results open the tea bag), and bread crumbs.

Vermicompost bins are best for addressing average kitchen scraps. Small bins will not be the best choice for composting meat, weeds, or large quantities of organic matter (e.g., paper plates from a big party).

Check the moisture level of your vermicompost bin regularly. The bedding should be kept damp at all times to keep your worms happy and snug in their home. If the bedding is getting dry, spritz with a spray bottle to moisten it.

If you notice that the bedding material is getting depleted, add new strips of damp newspaper to build it back up.

Around three months after you start your bin, when your container is filled with compost (known as worm castings), it's time to empty the bin. Two weeks beforehand, stop feeding the worms organic matter. At the end of the two-week period, collect the compost.

An easy method for collecting the compost is to spread out a clean plastic tarp or old plastic shower curtain on a flat, dry surface. Dump the contents of the vermicompost bin directly on the center of the tarp and shape it into a mound. The worms will head to the bottom of the mound to escape the light. When they do, remove the compost from the top of the mound and transfer it to a clean storage container. Mound the remaining material and repeat until only a shallow layer of compost is left along with your worms.

Fill your vermicompost container halfway with new moist newspaper strips. Gently sift the worms out of the remaining compost and return them to the fresh vermicompost bin environment along with any remaining organic scraps collected from the compost pile.

Use the collected compost for planting, store it for future use, or spread a fine layer around your garden areas.

Repeat the compost collection process every 3–4 months. In order to stay healthy, your worms will need to be separated from their castings regularly.

 Chick Tip: Make vermicompost tea for watering your plants. Add a cup of vermicompost to a gallon of water. Allow the mixture to rest or steep for twenty-four hours. Then use it for watering to refresh soil nutrients in your container plants.

START A GARDEN CLUB

Members of the garden club can also lend a helping hand to each other to ease the burden of heavy-duty harvest seasons, tend to each other's gardens when someone is traveling, and, best of all, have a garden buddy to chat with from time to time. Talking only to flowers and weeds can get a bit dull after a while.

Contact your local extension office, technology center, community centers, and library to see if a gardening club already exists in your area. If so, great—jump right in and say "Howdy!"

If a local club does not exist, offer to work with your extension agency or library to begin one (libraries offer terrific meeting spaces that are most often free to nonprofit clubs). Or reach out to a few of your neighbors or friends to see if they'd be interested in starting a weekly or monthly garden support group. When weather permits, rotate your meetings from garden to garden and use part of the time to help each other weed or spruce up the space. In the cold weather, meet indoors to browse over seed catalogues, share lessons from this year's crop, and develop planting plans for the next season. Design a fun project like decorating flower pots or making wreaths.

Take your group to the community by offering to help prepare and support a public garden or to aid fellow community members who may need a little helping hand. If you don't have the time for direct volunteer work, consider donating excess produce to local churches, or start a community website where gardeners can connect and ask questions of their fellow plant buffs.

5. Get Cured:

Preserving
Your Bounty

Now that you have an armful of fresh, lovely produce and a refrigerator full of eggs, you need to figure out a plan for keeping your goods in tip-top edible shape. Of course, fresh is best but, if you've played your sustainable cards right, you have an excess of goods to enjoy long after the harvest season and peak egg production are past.

All the techniques for preserving food stem from the very basic need to survive. Though we've developed modern methods, there's no denying that many of the original processes are still the most natural and effective ways of preserving food. Over time, all foods do lose some nutritional value when stored, but it's still far more satisfying to open a home-canned jar of salsa than to settle for a chemically laden product from the convenience store.

The goal of food preservation is to prevent food spoilage and the deterioration of food. Preserving your own food also has a significant impact on reducing both your grocery costs and your impact on the environment.

The key to success with food preservation methods is to begin with the proper equipment and with quality meat and produce. Avoid using foods that are bruised, molded, overripe, diseased, or have signs of insect damage. Prior to any food preservation method, all foods should also be washed and dried properly.

Proven preservation methods for common food types are:

- Cellaring
- Freezing
- Pressure Canning
- Pickling
- Alcohol Curing
- Drying
- Salt Curing
- Smoking

Recommended Preservation Methods by Food Type			
POULTRY	**EGGS**	**VEGETABLES**	**FRUITS**
Salt curing, smoking, freezing, pressure canning, drying (jerky)	Freezing, pickling	Cellaring, freezing, salt curing, pressure canning, alcohol canning, pickling, drying	Freezing, pressure canning, alcohol, pickling, drying

WHAT'S IN YOUR MYSTERY PACKAGE?

Clear labeling is the key to preserving food properly, safely, and effectively. While most packaging may allow you to clearly discern what is inside, it won't help you determine the expiration date or variation in contents. Serving hot salsa when your guest can tolerate only mild is a big snafu easily avoided with good labeling habits. Each label for your preserved goods should include:

- Name of the food
- Important attributes of the food, such as temperature (e.g., spicy, mild), flavoring (e.g., vanilla, bourbon), and style (e.g., chopped, pureed)
- Date food was processed

CELLARING—IT'S WHERE ROOT VEGETABLES GO TO CHILL

Root cellaring is perfect for carrots, turnips, potatoes, onions, shallots, garlic, pumpkins, and winter squash. Cellared items must be kept in a dry area with adequate airflow at cold temperatures but above freezing, around 40 degrees Fahrenheit. Because of this, cellaring is not an ideal project for apartment or condo living situations.

Prior to cellaring, all vegetables (except for potatoes) must be cured by exposing the harvest to warm temperatures for approximately two weeks prior to cellaring. A terrific space for curing these vegetables is a screened-in porch, though we have been known to lay garlic on screens and set them on top of the slide area of our sons' playground. Basically, the area needs to be exposed to hot temperatures and adequate air circulation for the two-week curing period.

Potatoes may be placed directly in a root cellar; however, they must be fully mature at the time of harvesting.

Carrots and turnips store well covered in sand or salt in five-gallon buckets. Both methods help preserve moisture in these vegetables. Add a thick layer of sand or salt, followed by a layer of vegetables, then another layer of sand or salt, and continue this pattern until the bucket is full. On top should be a thick layer of sand or salt. When vegetables are needed, simply dig in the sand or salt and pluck one out!

FREEZING—IT'S COLD BUT FRESH IN HERE

Freezing is an ideal way to preserve the nutrients, flavor and natural colors of meat, garden fruits and vegetables. If processed correctly with quality materials, frozen produce are the next best thing to fresh.

Basic Tenets for All Freezer Goods:

- Store all freezer goods at or below 0 degrees Fahrenheit.
- Allow space between packages for air circulation.
- Use moisture-proof wrapping materials and containers to prevent freezer burn.

- Clearly label containers with contents, amount, and date of freezing. Be sure to use waterproof ink.
- Freeze only fresh meat and well-ripened, fresh vegetables and fruits. Bruises may be cut out of vegetables or fruits prior to packaging but avoid freezing wilted, spotted, or overripe vegetables or fruits.
- Wash and drain meats, fruits, and vegetables thoroughly; remove feathers from poultry and insects from produce.
- Sort according to size, unless you are chopping or pureeing.

Bacteria, yeasts and molds are inactive at temperatures below 0 degrees Fahrenheit. Once thawed, however, they may reactivate. Thawed foods should be handled promptly and in the same manner as fresh.

Chick Tip: In the event of a power failure, if you keep the freezer door closed, food will stay frozen for up to two days. Use dry ice to keep food frozen if outage lasts more than two days.

Chick Tip: Most foods can be refrozen. If the food has defrosted in the refrigerator and kept at 40 degrees Fahrenheit, it is generally safe to refreeze. Check foodsafety.gov for the most up-to-date information on proper food storage.

Most fruits and vegetables are highly suitable for freezing, but there are a few exceptions that do not freeze well, including potatoes, pears, green onions, tomatoes, celery, lettuce, and radishes.

FREEZER POULTRY

Chickens, turkeys, and most other fowl may be frozen whole, halved, or pieced. The day prior to processing, meat should be butchered, plucked, cleaned, and chilled in the refrigerator overnight. Turkey should be chilled for two days.

Butcher paper or vacuum packaging may be used for whole, halved, and pieced poultry. Freezer containers are appropriate for pieced. If you plan to regularly freeze chicken, a vacuum sealer is ideal.

Before packaging, it's important to decide how you plan to use the meat. Will you be regularly roasting whole chickens or primarily cooking boneless chicken breasts and using legs and thighs for soups? This will help you decide on how much to wrap and how the poultry will be best frozen.

Giblets (heart, liver, gizzard) should be packaged separately from poultry parts. Freezing is the best method of preservation for giblets, and they may be frozen for up to four months. If you aren't a fan of giblets, cook them thoroughly, then chop and feed as a treat to your dogs or cats.

Use one of the following methods to package:

Butcher paper	Whole, halved, pieced	Spread out a sheet of butcher paper that is generous enough to wrap around all sides of the meat, leaving a 6-inch overlap. Place meat in center of paper, join opposite sides together and fold excess down and under. Repeat with open sides. Secure flaps with freezer tape. Label and stack packages in freezer for storage.
Vacuum packaging	Whole, halved, pieced, giblets	Follow manufacturer instructions to cut, vacuum, and seal edges of vacuum package. Label and stack packages in freezer for storage.
Freezer containers	Pieced, giblets	Arrange pieces in layers in freezer container, leaving a ½-inch headspace. Seal, label, and stack containers in freezer for storage.

To use for cooking, defrost in the refrigerator, use defrost setting on microwave, or submerge in a cold water bath. If you thaw using a cold water bath, continue to change water to keep it cold. Poultry should not be defrosted at room temperature.

 Chick Tip: If you find gray or white hard spots on frozen chicken, it's typically a result of freezer burn. When minimal, simply cut them out prior to cooking. If prominent, chicken may not be suitable for consumption and should be disposed of properly.

FREEZER CHICKEN STOCK
Yield: 2 Quarts

Ingredients:
Chicken bones and skin from 1
    chicken, raw or cooked
½ cup celery, chopped
½ cup onion, peeled and
    chopped
½ cup carrots, peeled and
    chopped
¼ cup fresh parsley, chopped
1 tsp. salt
1 tsp. black pepper, ground
12 cups water

In a large stock pot, over high heat, add all ingredients; stir gently to distribute evenly. Bring to a boil, and boil for 2 minutes. Reduce heat to low, and simmer uncovered for 4 hours. Every hour, skim foam off the top of the stock and discard it.

Remove from heat. Strain and reserve stock liquid. Cool liquid for ½ hour, then pour it into an airtight freezer container, leaving ½-inch headspace.

Optionally, store stock in ¼-cup portions for ease of use. Using standard-size muffin tins, measure out ¼ cup of chicken stock per muffin well. Set muffin tray in freezer (tray must lie flat on shelf), and freeze overnight or until stock is frozen. Remove chicken stock cubes from muffin tin, and place in an airtight freezer storage container. To help prevent them from freezing to each other, use wax paper between layers. When you need chicken stock, simply remove cubes to meet the measurement needed, e.g., 4 cubes equals 1 cup of chicken stock.

Stock may be stored in refrigerator for up to 1 week or frozen for up to 2 months.

FREEZER EGGS

The first rule of freezing eggs is that whole eggs in the shell should not be frozen. They can crack easily in the freezer, and when they are defrosted they'll be very rubbery and not suitable for cooking or baking.

On the other hand, raw eggs without the shell may be frozen for up to one year. Depending upon your needs, you can freeze the yolks separately from the whites, or scramble the eggs prior to freezing. Be sure to select only fresh eggs, free from debris.

You can pour egg matter straight into a freezer container (leaving a half-inch headspace), but I prefer to premeasure and prefreeze, using ice cube trays prior to placing in freezer containers for permanent storage. This makes it super-easy to grab the portion you need.

Step 1:

Whole Egg	Egg Whites	Egg Yolks
Crack eggs into a mixing bowl. Gently scramble (beat) yolks and whites together until fully blended.	Separate whites from yolks. In a mixing bowl, use a fork to gently blend whites together.	Separate egg yolks from white. In a mixing bowl, use a fork to gently blend yolks together. For every three egg yolks, add a tsp. of salt, and stir gently until fully incorporated.

Step 2:

Gently remove any air bubbles from egg mix. Portion mix individually into compartments of ice-cube tray using the following chart:

Whole Eggs	Egg Whites	Egg Yolks
3 Tbsp.	2 tbsp.	1 tbsp.

Freeze eggs in ice tray for 4 hours or until frozen solid. Remove egg "ice" from ice trays and immediately place in a freezer-safe container, leaving a half-inch headspace. If desired, add a layer of wax paper between egg layers for easier removal of cubes. Seal, label, and stack containers in freezer for storage.

Each cube will be the equivalent of its fresh egg counterpart. For example, one whole egg frozen cube is the equivalent of one fresh egg. To use for cooking, defrost egg cubes in a small bowl in the refrigerator.

FREEZER FRUITS

Fruits can be frozen using one of five methods: syrup, sugar, unsweetened, puree, or juice.

Fruit should be cleaned, dried, cored, and seeded, then halved, sliced, or chopped. For melons, rind must also be removed. Berries, cherries, and grapes may be canned whole, but any pits or seeds should be removed.

Fruit Preparation Methods for Freezing		
METHOD	FRUIT	DIRECTIONS
Simple Syrup Frozen Fruit Method (see recipe below)	Apple, blackberry, blueberry, cantaloupe, cherry, cranberry, grape, honeydew, peach, plum, raspberry, rhubarb, strawberry, watermelon	Add fruit to freezer container, cover with simple syrup, leaving a ½-inch headspace (fruit should be completely submerged). Immediately seal, label, and stack containers in freezer for storage.

Fruit Preparation Methods for Freezing		
Sugared Frozen Fruit Method	Apple, blackberry, cherry, peach, raspberry, strawberry	In a large mixing bowl, add fruit. Add ⅓ cup sugar per 1 cup fruit. Toss or stir to mix thoroughly. Pack fruit into a freezer container, leaving a ½-inch headspace. Immediately seal, label, and stack containers in freezer for storage.
Unsweetened Frozen Fruit Method	Apple, blackberry, blueberry, cherry, cranberry, grape, peach, plum, raspberry, rhubarb, strawberry	Lay fruit in a single layer on wax paper-lined trays, leaving a space between each fruit piece. Freeze for 1 hour. Remove fruit from freezer, and pack into a freezer container, leaving a ½-inch headspace. Immediately seal, label, and stack containers in freezer for storage.
Pureed Frozen Fruit Method	Blackberry, blueberry, cherry, cranberry, grape, peach, pear, plum, raspberry, strawberry	Remove skin from fruit, if needed. Using a food processor, puree fruit. If you wish to de-seed berries, press through a sieve. Ladle puree into a freezer container, leaving a ½-inch headspace. Immediately seal, label, and stack containers in freezer for storage.
Frozen Fruit Juice Method	Apple, cherry, grape, peach, plum, strawberry	Remove skins from fruit. Using a conventional slow juicer, juice fruit. If desired, mix ¼ to ½ cup sugar per quart of juice. Ladle juice into a freezer container, leaving a ½-inch headspace. Immediately seal, label, and stack containers in freezer for storage.

Chick Tip: Blackberries, raspberries, and blueberries may be juiced, but it's best to juice them fresh. Rhubarb may be pureed or juiced too, but must be boiled in water for three minutes to soften prior to pureeing or extracting juice.

SIMPLE SYRUP RECIPE

Yield: 5 cups

Ingredients:
3 cups sugar
4 cups water

In a medium saucepan, over medium-high heat, warm water until hot. Add sugar, stir to dissolve. Remove from heat, and cool completely prior to use.

QUICK & EASY APPLESAUCE

Makes 4–5 quarts

Ingredients:
16 cups apples, cored, peeled and
  chopped
1 cup sugar
1½ cups water
2 Tbsp. lemon juice

In a large saucepan over medium heat, add water, lemon juice, and apples. Cook, stirring occasionally until apples are tender. Remove from heat.

For chunky applesauce: In a large mixing bowl, add sugar and apples. Mash with a fork or masher until sugar is combined and chunky applesauce is formed.

For smooth applesauce: Using a food processor, puree apples. In a large mixing bowl, add puree and sugar, and mix until sugar is dissolved into applesauce.

Ladle applesauce into freezer containers, leaving a ½-inch headspace. Seal, label, and stack containers in freezer for storage.

Applesauce Variations	
Cinnamon Applesauce	Add 2 Tbsp. cinnamon to apples prior to cooking.
Spiced Applesauce	Add 1 Tbsp. cinnamon, 1 Tsp. Nutmeg, and 1 Tbsp. allspice to apples prior to cooking.
Mulled Applesauce	Swap ½ cup water with ½ cup of orange juice. Add 1 tsp. cinnamon, ½ tsp. ground ginger and ¼ tsp. ground cloves to apples prior to cooking.
Berry Applesauce	Reduce apples by 2 cups prior to cooking. When apples are fully cooked, stir in 2 cups of pureed (and de-seeded if preferred) berries. Proceed with mashing or puree process.

FREEZER VEGGIES

For the bulk of vegetables, blanching is the key to your ultimate success. Blanching is the process of briefly boiling vegetables, then quickly cooling them, to preserve flavor and color. Blanching stops the growth of the vegetable, which helps avoid discoloration, toughening, loss of nutrients, and loss of flavor for freezer storage. Blanching also wilts and softens the vegetable, making it more flexible for packaging.

The rule of thumb for blanching is to use one gallon of boiling water per one pound of vegetables. Water should be heated using a traditional blancher with blanching basket and lid or by using a large stock pot with a wire basket and lid.

Make sure the vegetables for blanching are clean, dry, bug-free, and (if desired) chopped.

BLANCHING 101

Heat water in a large stock pot (or blancher) until boiling.

While water is heating, prepare a cooling station with a strainer and a large mixing bowl. Fill the mixing bowl one-third full of ice then top with cold water until the bowl is half-full with the ice water mix.

When water is boiling blanch vegetables for the time recommended on the blanching chart on page 103. Remove from heat immediately, strain, and plunge strained vegetables into the ice water mix. Continue to add ice and cold water until vegetables are completely cooled.

Remove vegetables from water, drain, and dry. Pack vegetables into freezer container leaving a half-inch headspace. Immediately seal, label, and stack containers in freezer for storage.

Alternatively, pack vegetables into vacuum freezer storage bags and vacuum seal according to manufacturer directions. Immediately label and stack bags in freezer for storage.

Vegetable	Minutes to Blanch
Asparagus, small	2
Asparagus, large	4
Broccoli, whole	5
Broccoli, pieces	3
Brussels sprouts	5
Carrots, whole	5
Carrots, diced	2
Cauliflower	3
Corn, cob	10
Corn, cut	4
Green beans	2
Kale	2
Lima beans	4
Okra	4
Peas, shelled	2
Peas, sugar snap	3
Spinach	1
Squash, cut into pieces	3
Yellow wax beans	2

FREEZING PEPPERS

Bell Peppers: Wash, seed, and stem. Cut in half or slice. Pack peppers into freezer container leaving a half-inch headspace. Immediately seal, label, and stack containers in freezer for storage.

Alternatively, pack peppers into vacuum freezer storage bags and vacuum seal according to manufacturer directions. Immediately label, and stack bags in freezer for storage.

Hot Peppers: Wash and stem. Pack peppers into freezer container, placing a small square of wax paper between each layer of peppers (this makes it super easy to use one or two peppers when needed, rather than defrosting the entire container). Leave a half-inch headspace. Immediately seal, label, and stack containers in freezer for storage.

Alternatively, pack peppers into vacuum freezer storage bags and vacuum seal according to manufacturer directions. Immediately label and stack bags in freezer for storage.

 Chick Tip: Fresh herbs can easily be frozen, ice cube style, to be used for recipes or in refreshments. Rosemary or sage ice cubes are lovely in lemonade! Mix 1 cup of chopped fresh herbs with 1 cup of water, pour into a clean ice cube tray, and freeze for 8 hours. To use for a recipe, remove herb ice cubes needed and thaw in a bowl at room temperature. Herb ice cubes may be stored in the freezer up to six months.

CANNING: THE BEST WAY TO EXPRESS YOUR LOVE OF MASON JARS

Canning is a joyful process that's actually rather easy to do. However, there are so many variables to the process that is impossible to address every facet adequately in a limited chapter segment. We will, however, address all the basics to get you started on your journey to creating fun and delicious recipes.

There are two basic methods of canning: boil-water processing and steam-pressure processing.

Boil-Water Processing	Steam-Pressure Processing
Foods are processed at 212 degrees Fahrenheit	Foods are processed at 240 degrees Fahrenheit
Preferred canning method for most fruits, pickles and tomatoes	Preferred canning method for most vegetables and meats
Uses boiling water to process	Uses water steam pressure to process
Requires a boiling-water canner	Requires a steam pressure canner, which may often double as a boiling-water canner

The biggest health concern with canning is botulism, a poisonous toxin caused by the germination of botulism spores, a naturally present substance in our environment. Following proper canning techniques and canning at the proper temperatures will destroy botulism spores and toxins.

If after canning a lid does not seal, the canned goods should be reprocessed if possible or refrigerated and consumed within one week. If after canning a canned good shows any sign of spoilage, looks strange, or smells strange upon opening, the food should be properly destroyed and not consumed.

If you suspect foods are spoiled, do not feed foods to animals or compost. Food should be burned or hard-boiled, cooled down and then discarded as standard waste.

A SUSTAINABLE CHICK'S CANNING EQUIPMENT INVENTORY:

- **Pressure-Cooker and Canner**, preferably one with the ability to double as a boiling-water canner.
- **Mason Jars** in pint and quart size in standard and wide-mouth styles. Jelly jar sizes are nice for aesthetics, but a simple wide-mouth pint jar will suffice (and look just as cute when dolled up with ribbon, cloth, and labels!).
- **Lids, Rings and Seals for Jars**. These items may be purchased separately or in kits. Also consider reusable combination lids with built-in seals. The upfront cost is slightly higher, but the amortized cost is lower. As a bonus, some reusable lids are made using recycled materials, boosting your environmental green power.
- **Canning Tongs**. Of all the extra gadgets available, canning tongs make the top of my list. Preformed to easily grab and grip the neck of the Mason jar, these tongs prevent many a scorched finger and broken bottle.
- **Funnels**, one for wide-mouth jars and one for standard. This is not a necessity, but you'll be thankful you have it when it comes time to fill the jars. Funnels help prevent splatters and keep the rim and outside of the jars cleaner during the filling process.
- **Gap Measuring Stick.** If you are new to canning, it's difficult to gauge what a half-inch headspace looks like. This measuring stick will save you from estimating incorrectly, which can lead to improper processing and/or spoilage.
- **Ladle.** A sturdy ladle, ideally with a small pouring lip built in, is a must-have for ladling hot liquid into jars. It's also a terrific tool to have around for use with soups and stews.
- **Magnetic Lid Grabber.** A luxury, but a great one to have when trying to quickly extract lids and rims from hot-water baths.
- **Cooling Rack.** Special canning racks are available, but a simple, sturdy baker's rack will suffice.

Pre-Canning Prep for boiling-water processing and steam-pressure processing:

1. Inspect canning jars, lids, rings, seals, and equipment for cracks, flaws, or repairs. Remove any cracked or flawed pieces from your canning inventory and repurpose, recycle, or discard. Make repairs as needed.
2. Clean and sterilize canning jars, lids, rings, seals, and equipment.
3. Prep food for recipe (i.e., dice, cut, wash, dry).
4. Inspect food for signs of spoilage, disease, or insect damage. If minimal, remove blemished spots. If prevalent, dispose of foods properly. Only use ripe, disease-free, insect-free, and otherwise spoilage-free foods for canning.
5. Prepare work area for canning. Clean and sterilize sink or large basin for hot packing.
6. Proceed with steps for boiling-water canning method or steam-pressure canning method as appropriate.

BOILING-WATER CANNING METHOD

1. Fill boiling-water canner with water according to manufacturer's instructions. Water should be adequate to cover jars with two inches of water. A two-inch airspace should be left at the top of the canner to prevent the pot from boiling over.
2. Preheat water to hot, but do not boil.
3. While water is heating, prepare recipe per instructions.
4. Prepare jars, lids, and rings for filling by soaking them in a hot, sterile water bath. Jars should always be kept hot for filling when pouring hot ingredients or boiling water into them. If the glass is not prewarmed, you run the risk of breakage.
5. Fill jars, leaving appropriate headspace per recipe directions. Gently break up any air bubbles in liquids (a butter knife works well for this task). Wipe rims and adjust seals according to manufacturer's directions.
6. Set jars in boiling-water canner rack. Jars should not be touching. Set rack in boiling-water canner.
7. Remove excess water, if needed, to ensure a two-inch headspace in canner. Jars

should be covered by two inches of water; excess may be removed.

8. Place lid on canner and bring to a boil. When water reaches a full boil, begin timing per recipe requirements.

9. After processing for recommended time, remove jars from canner, and set on cooling rack for twelve hours or until jars are completely cool to touch.

10. Clean jars of any residue, and check to make sure all jars have sealed properly. Store in pantry, cellar, or other cool, dry, dark location.

STEAM-PRESSURE CANNING METHOD

Follow steps for boiling-water canning method with the following exceptions for steps 7 through 10:

A reduced amount of water is used in steam-pressure canning. Follow manufacturer's instructions for filling steam-pressure canner with water and heating.

Instead of bringing the water to a boil to process the food, steam pressure is built up within the pressure cooker. When the appropriate amount of pressure is built up, the timing process begins.

Pressure canners must be watched and regulated throughout the process to keep the temperature at a steady heat and pressure at a safe level. This is achieved by decreasing or increasing the heat and releasing steam through the pressure valve.

When pressure canners have finished processing, the entire canner is removed from the heat and allowed to cool. The lid should not be removed before the pressure is fully reduced, and, even then, extra precautions should be taken when removing the lid to prevent scalding and burns. Always follow the manufacturer's guide for all procedures to avoid injury.

Chick Tip: To enhance your canning joy, experience, and knowledge base, I highly recommend downloading and reading the USDA Complete Guide to Home Canning (nchfp.uga.edu/publications/publications_usda.html). This guide will serve as an excellent resource and provide you with plenty of additional recipe inspiration too.

Chick Tip: Altitude makes a difference in canning times. Consult the National Center for Food Preservation (nchfp.uga.edu) for conversion charts to ensure food safety standards are met.

OLD-WORLD IRISH MINCEMEAT
Yield: 6 quarts

In keeping with her Irish traditions and roots, every Thanksgiving and Christmas (and sometimes on Easter), my Grandma Mary would bake amazing mincemeat pies. The problem with Old World recipes and Old World cooks, though, is that everything comes down to a pinch of this and a pinch of that—if you can even pry the secret recipe from them, that is! I did my best to duplicate my grandma's style in my version of mincemeat pie filling. I think she'd approve!

Ingredients:
1 cup raisins
1 cup currants
1 cup white seedless grapes
1 cup beef suet, shredded
*2 cups apples, peeled, cored, and
    diced*
2 cups brown sugar
¼ cup orange rind, grated
¼ cup orange juice
½ cup almonds, sliced
*½ cup candied (glazed) mixed
    peel*
½ cup spiced rum
2 tsp. nutmeg, ground
1 tsp. allspice
1 tsp. cinnamon

In a large mixing bowl, add raisins, apples, currants, almonds, suet, and orange rind, and mixed peel. Toss to mix well. Add brown sugar, nutmeg, cinnamon, and allspice. Toss to mix well. Add orange juice and rum, and stir until fully combined.

Pour mixture into a Dutch oven. Cook over medium heat until mixture comes to a boil. Reduce heat and simmer for 15 minutes, stirring frequently.

Ladle warm mincemeat into quart jars, leaving a 1-inch headspace. Process in pressure cooker at 10 lbs. pressure for 90 minutes.

PEAR BASIL PRESERVES

Yield: 4 pints

Ingredients:
8 cups Bartlett pears, peeled,
  cored, and chopped fine
1 cup honey
1 cup sugar
¼ cup lemon peel, grated
½ cup lemon juice
1 Tbsp. fresh basil, chopped fine

In a large saucepan over medium heat, add pears, honey, sugar, lemon juice, and peel. Stir until fully mixed. Increase heat to medium-high and bring to a boil, stirring frequently. Add basil and reduce heat to low. Simmer for 25 minutes, stirring frequently. Remove from heat.

Ladle warm pear preserves into pint jars, leaving a ½-inch headspace. Process in boiling-water canner 10 minutes (from boiling point).

BLACKBERRY WINE JELLY

Yield: 2 pints

Ingredients:
2 cups blackberries, pureed and
  seeded (if preferred)
1 cup red table wine
1 cup sugar
3 Tbsp. Ball RealFruit Classic
  Pectin

In a large saucepan, over medium heat, add blackberries and wine. Slowly stir in pectin. Continue stirring gently until pectin is fully absorbed.

Turn heat on stovetop to high. Bring wine mixture to a boil, stirring constantly. Add sugar, stir until completely dissolved. Continue stirring and return to a hard boil. Hard boil for one minute, stirring continuously. Remove from heat. Skim foam off the top of liquid and discard.

Ladle hot jelly into pint or jelly jars, leaving a ¼-inch headspace. Process in boiling-water canner 10 minutes (from boiling point).

ORCHARD FRUIT JELLY

Yield: 3 pints

Ingredients:

2 cups grapes, pureed and
  seeded
1 cup peach, pureed
½ cup fresh orange juice
¼ cup fresh apple juice
2 Tbsp. fresh lemon juice
2 Tbsp. lime juice
1 cup sugar
3 Tbsp. Ball RealFruit Classic
  Pectin

In a large saucepan, over medium heat, add purees and juices. Slowly stir in pectin. Continue stirring gently until pectin is fully absorbed.

Turn heat on stove top to high. Bring fruit mixture to a boil, stirring constantly. Add sugar, stir until completely dissolved. Continue stirring and return to a hard boil. Hard boil for one minute, stirring continuously. Skim foam off the top of liquid and discard. Remove from heat.

Ladle hot jelly into pint or jelly jars, leaving a ¼-inch headspace. Process in boiling-water canner 10 minutes (from boiling point).

TOMATILLO TART SALSA

Yield: 2 pints

Ingredients:

4 cups tomatillos, husked, cored and diced

2 cups Granny Smith apples, peeled, cored and diced

½ cup red bell pepper, seeded and diced

¼ cup jalapeno pepper, seeded and diced thin

½ cup fresh cilantro, chopped thin

½ cup apple cider vinegar

In a large saucepan over medium heat, add all ingredients, stir until fully mixed and warmed. Increase heat to high, bring to a boil, stirring frequently. Boil for 1 minute. Reduce heat to low and simmer for 20 minutes.

Ladle salsa into pint jars, leaving a ½-inch headspace. Process in boiling-water canner 10 minutes (from boiling point).

STRAWBERRY DAIQUIRI JAM
Yield 4 pints.

Ingredients:

*4 cups strawberries, capped and
    crushed*
½ cup lime juice
¼ cup lime peel, grated
½ cup white rum
2 cups sugar
*3 Tbsp. Ball RealFruit Classic
    Pectin*

In a large saucepan, over medium heat, add strawberries, lime juice, lime peel, and rum. Slowly stir in pectin. Continue stirring gently until pectin is fully absorbed.

Turn heat on stovetop to high. Bring mixture to a boil, stirring constantly. Add sugar, stir until completely dissolved. Continue stirring and return to a hard boil. Hard boil for one minute, stirring continuously. Remove from heat. Skim foam off the top of liquid and discard.

Ladle hot jam into pint or jelly jars, leaving a ¼-inch headspace. Process in boiling-water canner 10 minutes (from boiling point).

ORANGE TANGERINE MARMALADE

Yield: 4 pints

Ingredients:

1½ *cups orange peel, chopped*
    thin
½ *cup tangerine peel, chopped*
    thin
3 *cups oranges, peeled, seeded*
    and chopped
1 *cup tangerines, peeled, seeded*
    and chopped
1 *cup lemon, peeled, seeded and*
    chopped
6 *cups sugar*
6 *cups water*

In a large stockpot, over a low heat, add orange peel, tangerine peel, oranges, tangerines, lemon, and water. Simmer for 10 minutes, stirring occasionally. Remove from heat. Cover and set aside in a cool, dry spot overnight (10–12 hours).

Return pot to stove, uncover and cook over medium heat until peel is soft. Increase heat to high, add sugar, stirring continuously until sugar is fully incorporated and dissolved. Bring to boil, stirring continuously until liquid begins to gel. Remove from heat.

Ladle hot marmalade into pint or jelly jars, leaving a ¼-inch headspace. Process in boiling-water canner 10 minutes (from boiling point).

ALCOHOL CANNING: THE FORGOTTEN PROCESS

Once upon a time, canning with alcohol was common, but the use faded when more modern techniques like pressure canning and freezing took over. "Drunken fruit" became a delicacy, rather than a norm. The immediate benefit of canning with alcohol is that alcohol is a bacterial deterrent. The drawback is that the shelf life is shorter, as fruit soaked in alcohol may begin to ferment in excess after six months of storage, which may sour the mix. As with any preservation method, always watch for signs of spoilage, and promptly discard any fruit that exhibits signs of spoilage, such as mold or suspect odors.

Canning with alcohol is one of my favorite methods, as it allows for development of new complexities in flavor and certainly adds interest to any pie or dessert you may use the fruit for! One of my very favorite things to can with alcohol and the one I use the most often is vanilla extract. It's so easy to create and maintain a steady stream of pure vanilla extract, which yields superior results to store-purchased varieties. Give it a try, and I think you'll soon be hooked on the merits of alcohol canning!

PURE VANILLA EXTRACT
Yield: 1 quart

Ingredients:
3 vanilla beans
1 cup vodka

Lay vanilla beans on a flat, clean, dry surface. With a paring knife, starting one inch from the top of the bean, make a small cut along the outer surface lengthwise. Stop the cut one inch from the opposite end of the bean.

Place the split vanilla beans in a sterile quart-size jar. Fill jar with vodka, leaving a ½-inch headspace. If necessary, press the vanilla beans down to ensure they are fully covered with alcohol. Cap the jar with an airtight seal. Store in a cool, dark, dry location for one month prior to use. Once per week during the first month's storage, gently swish the contents of the jar, then return the jar to the shelf.

After one month's storage, the pure vanilla extract will be potent enough to use in recipes. Always keep the vanilla beans submerged by adding additional vodka when needed. Store for up to one year, then remove old vanilla beans and add new split vanilla beans. You can continue this method perpetually for an unlimited supply of pure vanilla extract.

If you prefer a vanilla bourbon extract, swap out the vodka with quality bourbon.

Plenty of fruit, but where's the rum?

Fruit soaked in alcohol is fabulous for using as a drink garnish or a topper for ice cream, pound cake, yogurt, ricotta, or brownies. It's also a marvelous twist to use in place of fresh fruit in your standard recipes. Whatever recipe you would normally use fruit for, such as muffins or tarts, you can substitute fruit canned with alcohol.

The process is quite simple. Pack quality, clean, dry, fresh whole fruits or sliced fruits in a wide-mouth sterile quart jar, then top with the alcohol of your choice, leaving a half-inch headspace. Always be sure to completely submerge the fruit in the alcohol. Cap the jar with an airtight seal and store in a cool, dark, dry location to marinate for at least one month prior to use. Store for up to six months.

Need a little inspiration? Try one of these flavor sensations:

Sliced and pitted peaches	+	Brandy
Sliced and pitted plums	+	Maple whiskey
Pitted Bing cherries	+	Bourbon
Sliced and de-seeded oranges	+	Vodka
Sliced and pitted nectarines	+	Spiced rum
Capped and sliced strawberries	+	Moonshine
Raspberries	+	Vanilla vodka
Blackberries	+	Bourbon
Sliced and pitted apricots	+	Ouzo
Cranberries	+	Gin
Sliced, cored, and seeded pears	+	Brandy
Sliced and seeded limes	+	Tequila

 Chick Tip: Most recipes will call for draining the fruit from the alcohol base, but don't discard the liquid. The remaining alcohol will become a fabulous cordial that can be served as an after-dinner drink or used in place of your favorite spirits to create a truly unique custom cocktail for your next gathering.

DRUNKEN FRUIT COBBLER

Yield: Serves 4–6

Ingredients:

2 cups alcohol marinated fruit,
     drained
1 cup all-purpose flour
1 cup milk
1 cup sugar
½ cup butter, melted
½ tsp. nutmeg
½ tsp. cinnamon

Preheat oven to 375 degrees Fahrenheit.

In an 8 x 8-inch baking dish, add flour, milk, nutmeg, and cinnamon; stir until thoroughly mixed. Add melted butter; stir until fully mixed. (Cobbler crust will have a liquid consistency.) Spoon fruit evenly over cobbler crust. Bake for 1 hour or until crust is golden brown. Remove from oven, cool on a baker's rack for 10 minutes, then serve. Cobbler may also be served cold, if desired.

DRUNKEN FRUIT WHIPPED PIE

Yield: Serves 8–10

Ingredients:

2 cups alcohol-marinated fruit,
     drained
2 cups heavy whipped cream
1½ cups graham crackers,
     crushed
¼ cup sugar
⅓ cup butter, melted
½ tsp. cinnamon, ground

Preheat oven to 375 degrees Fahrenheit.

In a medium mixing bowl, add graham cracker crumbs, sugar, cinnamon, and melted butter. Stir until thoroughly mixed.

In an 8-inch pie pan, evenly spread graham cracker mix. Press to form a solid crust. Bake for 8–10 minutes or until crust is lightly browned. Remove from oven; cool on baker's rack for 1 hour.

In a large mixing bowl, add fruit and whipped cream. Beat until fully combined. Spoon fruit mix into cooled pie shell. Refrigerate for 1 hour prior to serving.

DRUNKEN FRUIT GALETTES

Yield: Serves 4-6

Ingredients:

3 cups alcohol marinated fruit, drained

2 cups all-purpose flour

¾ cup butter

½ tsp. salt

⅓ cups water

1 Tbsp. coarse sugar (decorating sugar)

In a large mixing bowl, add flour and salt; stir to mix. Add butter. Using a pastry cutter, cut butter into flour until fully crumbed. Add water slowly, stirring constantly, until a soft ball of dough is formed.

Transfer dough to a floured pastry sheet. Use a lightly floured rolling pin to gently flatten dough to ½-inch thickness. Chill dough in the refrigerator for 30 minutes.

Remove the dough from the refrigerator, cut the disk into 6 equal pieces. Lightly flour a work surface and roll each piece of dough into a small ball. Use a lightly floured rolling pin to gently flatten dough to ¼-inch thickness.

Grease two 9 x 13-inch glass baking pans. Transfer one galette round into one of the baking pans. Fold up the edges of the dough to form a bowl for the fruit, pleating sides to secure. Spoon ½ cup fruit into the center of the galette round. Fold the top of the dough atop the fruit, leaving an open space in the center. Repeat, placing each galette in a pan, leaving a one inch space between each galette.

Chill galettes in the refrigerator for 30 minutes.

Preheat oven to 400 degrees Fahrenheit.

Remove galettes from the refrigerator; bake for 35-40 minutes (or until crust is lightly browned). Remove from oven, cool pans on a wire baking rack for 15 minutes, then serve galettes. Galettes may also be served cold, if preferred.

TRADITIONAL LIMONCELLO
Yield: 2 quarts.

This popular Italian liqueur is perfect for sippin' on a breezy summer night. It's also fabulous when mixed with iced tea on a hot summer day.

Ingredients:

2 cups lemon peel
4 cups vodka
3 cups sugar
2 cups water

Sterilize two 1-quart Mason jars. Add 1 cup lemon peel to each jar. Pour 2 cups vodka over lemon peel in each jar. Cover tightly. Shake jar lightly, then store in a dark, cool, and dry place such as a pantry shelf for 2 weeks. Once per day, during the 2-week period, shake the jar gently and return to shelf.

When 2-week resting period is over, strain lemon peel from the vodka, reserving the vodka. Pour vodka back into quart jars in equal amounts. Set aside.

In a medium saucepan over high heat, add water and sugar. Bring to a boil, stirring constantly. Boil for 1 minute. Remove simple syrup from heat. Cool on a baking rack for 1 hour.

Pour syrup, in equal amounts, over vodka in quart jars. Stir gently until fully combined. Cover tightly, store in refrigerator for 24 hours prior to serving. May be transferred to smaller jars, if desired, and stored in refrigerator for up to 1 month.

RUM POT (RUMTOPF)

Yield: 4 quarts

The exact origins of *Rumtopf*, which translates into "rum pot," are a little unclear, with credit to both Holland and Germany. Wherever this preservation process originally took place, it's a wonderful holiday tradition that deserves to be preserved!

My method is a little more modern-world, with the use of quart jars and the placement of all fruit into the jars at one time. If you want to stay true to the Old World, stoneware Rumtopf pots to which you can add fruits seasonally are available at specialty stores.

Ingredients:
14 cups fresh fruits, washed and
dried (see list)
100-proof (or higher) dark rum
Sugar

Line up four sterile quart-size wide-mouth Mason jars. Select a fruit to begin with and add a 1-inch layer at the bottom of each jar. Sprinkle a little sugar on top of the layer. Add the next fruit layer and sprinkle a little sugar on top. Continue layering fruits until the Mason jars are full, with a minimum of a 2-inch headspace remaining. Pour rum over fruits, completely submerging the fruit, leaving a ½-inch headspace. Cap each jar with an airtight seal.

Store in a cool, dark, dry location for 1 month; then unseal and serve in a bowl with a dollop of fresh whipped cream. Rumtopf may also be used as a topping for ice cream, cake, cheesecake, crepes, or other baked goods.

Unopened Rumtopf may be stored in a cool, dark, dry location for up to 3 months. Opened Rumtopf may be stored in the refrigerator for up to 1 month.

Ideal fruit choices for a rum pot are:

- Apricots, pitted and quartered
- Blackberries
- Blueberries
- Cherries, pitted
- Grapes, seedless
- Peaches, pitted and quartered
- Pineapple, cut from rind, cored and cubed
- Plums, pitted and quartered
- Raspberries
- Strawberries, capped

PICKLING—GET YOUR PRODUCE TO PUCKER UP!

Pickled vegetables and relishes add a variety of flavor-filled options for sandwiches, dips, and sides. Summer squash, corn, cantaloupe, watermelon rind, beets, onions, eggs, and, of course, cucumbers are all popular items to pickle. Vinegar and salt are the key preserving components in pickling.

Apple vinegar or white vinegar may be used for any pickling recipe. The choice is really a matter of personal preference. Apple vinegar generally offers a little more tang and personality to your pickled goods, while white vinegar allows the attributes of the pickled items to shine through a bit more.

QUICK & EASY SANDWICH PICKLES

Yield: 2 quarts

There's nothing fancy about this tried-and-true recipe—it simply delivers speedy, great-tasting results! If you prefer a tart pickle over a sweet one, omit or reduce the sugar.

Ingredients:
6 cups cucumbers, sliced thin
1 cup onion, sliced
1 cup red bell pepper, sliced
2 cups sugar
1 cup white vinegar
1 Tbsp. salt

In a medium saucepan over medium heat, add vinegar, sugar, and salt. Bring to a boil, stirring occasionally, until sugar is fully dissolved. Remove from heat.

In a large mixing bowl, add cucumbers, onion, and pepper. Gently stir until well mixed. Pour vinegar mix over cucumber mix; stir gently. Ladle cucumbers into sterile wide-mouth quart jars, leaving a half-inch headspace. Pour any remaining vinegar mix into jars. Cap jars and store in refrigerator. For best results, allow jars to sit in the refrigerator for 48 hours prior to opening and serving. Store in refrigerator for up to 1 month.

PICKLED ONIONS

Yield: 1 quart

Ingredients:

*4 cups Vidalia or red onions,
    peeled, halved, and sliced*

3 cups white vinegar

2 cups water

4 bay leaves

1 tsp. allspice

¼ cup mustard seed

¼ cup sugar

In a medium saucepan over high heat, add vinegar, bay leaves, allspice, mustard seed, sugar, and water. Bring to a boil, stirring regularly. Remove from heat.

Fill pint jars with onion slices, leaving a 1-inch headspace. Ladle hot vinegar mix over onions, leaving a half-inch headspace. Cool jars on baking rack for 4 hours. Seal and store in the refrigerator for up to 1 month. For best results, allow jars to sit in the refrigerator for 48 hours prior to opening and serving. Store in refrigerator for up to 1 month.

OLD BAY VODKA CORN RELISH

Yield: 6 pints

Ingredients:

8 cups corn, cut and cooked
4 cups cabbage, chopped
1 cup white onion, peeled and
  chopped
2 cups red bell pepper, capped,
  seeded and chopped
2 cups sugar
3 cups white vinegar
2 cups vodka
¼ cup Old Bay seasoning
1 Tbsp. celery seed
1 Tbsp. mustard seed

In a large saucepan over medium-high heat, add all ingredients. Bring to a boil, stirring frequently. Boil for 2 minutes. Reduce heat to low, simmer for 15 minutes. Remove from heat.

Ladle relish into pint jars, leaving ¼-inch headspace. Cool jars on baking rack for 4 hours. Seal and store in the refrigerator for up to 1 month. For best results, allow jars to sit in the refrigerator for 48 hours prior to opening and serving.

For longer shelf storage, process in boiling-water canner 15 minutes (from boiling point).

BABY PICKLED WATERMELON
Yield: 4 pints

Use this recipe when you realize that you've planted an excess of watermelon or when the watermelon vines are blooming in abundance. For best results, pick baby watermelons within a week after the blossom falls off.

Ingredients:
4 cups (or 32 ounces) baby watermelons
2 cups apple cider vinegar
4 cups water
1 cup sugar
½ cup pickling salt
2 Tbsp. lemon zest
2 cinnamon sticks

In a large bowl, add 3 cups of water and salt; stir until salt is dissolved. Add baby watermelons to bowl. Allow watermelons to sit in brine for 24 hours, stirring occasionally to ensure brine is absorbed by the full surface area of the watermelon.

Remove watermelons from brine and rinse thoroughly with cold water.

In a large saucepan over medium-high heat, add 1 cup of water, vinegar, sugar, lemon zest, and cinnamon sticks. Bring to a boil, stirring frequently. Boil for 2 minutes. Reduce heat to low, add watermelons, and simmer for 15 minutes. Remove from heat.

Ladle watermelons into pint jars; top with liquid leaving a quarter-inch headspace. Cool jars on baking rack for 4 hours. Seal and store in the refrigerator for up to 1 month. For best results, allow jars to sit in the refrigerator for 48 hours prior to opening and serving.

For longer shelf storage, process in boiling-water canner 15 minutes (from boiling point).

CHERRY TOMATO TOMATILLO CHUTNEY
Yield: 6 pints

Ingredients:

*10 cups cherry tomatoes, peeled
    and quartered*
4 cups tomatillos, chopped
*2 cups cucumber, peeled and
    chopped*
1 cup Vidalia onion, chopped
*1 cup red bell pepper, seeded and
    chopped*
1 cup golden raisins
1 cup brown sugar
1 clove garlic, minced
1 Tbsp. ginger, minced
3 cups white vinegar

In a large stockpot over medium heat, add all ingredients. Stir frequently until warmed. Reduce heat to low and simmer until chutney is thick, stirring regularly. Remove from heat.

Ladle chutney into pint jars leaving ¼-inch headspace. Cool jars on baking rack for 2 hours. Seal and store in the refrigerator for up to 1 month. For best results, allow jars to sit in the refrigerator for 24 hours prior to opening and serving.

For longer shelf storage, process in boiling-water canner 10 minutes (from boiling point).

SALT CURING AND SMOKING—THE ANCIENT ART OF PRESERVATION

Salt curing is one of the oldest methods of preserving. As the name implies, salt is the primary ingredient used to cure the meat for long-term storage. Smoking is also an ancient technique for preserving meat that utilizes heat and smoke to cure or cook the meat indirectly.

Various methods of smoking include:

Dry Smoking	Dehydrating or drying out the meat while adding a smoky flavor
Cold Smoking	Salt curing by packing the meat in a salt rub or brining the meat using water and salt
Hot Smoking	Using coals, electric, or gas heat to heat and smoke the meat
Barbecue	Using a grill, fire pit, or other form of direct heat to cook the meat and (optionally) smoke the meat

As smoking is a slow process, older or less tender cuts of meat are well suited and will improve in flavor and tenderness as a result. The standard, recommended smoker temperature to be maintained is between 250 and 300 degrees Fahrenheit. Any lower or higher will result in potential harmful bacterial growth or drying of the meat. A 10–12-hour period is generally required for the smoking process.

Deciding on the type of smoker to use will be highly dependent upon your long-term objectives and housing limitations. Types of smokers available include charcoal-fueled, wood-fueled, wood pellet-fueled, gas, and electric. A variety of sizes and styles are available to suit your needs and space restrictions. Homemade smokers fashioned from wood and steel materials are also a viable option; just be sure to obtain plans for building from a reliable resource and to check with your local county and city offices regarding zoning laws.

Pit roasting is another form of smoking that requires a bit of work and inge-nuity but can be a fun option for large gatherings and picnics. A large hole dug into the earth serves as the cooking space for pit roasting. A hardwood fire is built into the pit and burnt until the wood is reduced to coals.

Barbecue grills and basic water pan smokers with domed lids are economical and easy choices to begin with. Both are obtainable through standard retail outlets. If you already own a backyard grill, it's a great place to start to decide if you like the flavoring and results from smoking chickens.

The most common method of salt curing poultry is brining. Brining is steeping the meat in a brine solution consisting primarily of salt and water to help improve the flavor of the meat, make the meat tenderer, and reduce moisture loss. This process extends the refrigerator life of raw chicken to up to two weeks. It's a great method to use when you have more chicken that you will reasonably use in a 3–4 day period and you do not wish to freeze it or preserve by another method.

Prior to brining, select, clean, and dry chickens that are fresh with no broken bones, discoloration, feathers, or bruises.

BASIC WET BRINE FOR CHICKEN

Ingredients:
1 whole chicken
*3 gallons of cold water (40
    degrees Fahrenheit)*
4 cups pickling salt
2 cups brown sugar

Optional additions to brine:
½ cup black pepper, ground
½ cup lemon pepper, ground
½ cup fresh basil, chopped
½ cup fresh rosemary, chopped
½ cup fresh oregano, chopped
½ cup fresh thyme, chopped
½ cup orange peel, sliced
½ cup lemon peel, sliced
4 cloves garlic, minced

In a 5-gallon stock pot, add water, salt, and brown sugar; stir until fully combined. Submerge chicken in pot to brine. Water should cover the chicken completely; if it does not, add more cold water until completely submerged. If the chicken does not stay submerged, use a safe item, such as a ceramic plate, to help weight the chicken.

Place stock pot in the refrigerator or another cool location with a temperature at or below 40 degrees Fahrenheit. To meet food safety standards, the brine needs to be kept at 40 degrees Fahrenheit at all times through the brining process.

Brine chicken for 1 day per pound or up to 3 days total. Each day, turn the chicken over to ensure all parts are being brined equally.

Remove poultry from brine and discard brine. Store chicken in refrigerator for up to 1 week, freezer pack chicken, or cook chicken per normal methods.

BASIC DRY BRINE FOR CHICKEN

Ingredients:
1 whole chicken
1 Tbsp. pickling salt per 5 lbs. of
  chicken

Optional additions to brine:
½ cup black pepper, ground
½ cup lemon pepper, ground
½ cup fresh basil, chopped fine
½ cup fresh rosemary, chopped
  fine
½ cup fresh oregano, chopped
  fine
½ cup fresh thyme, chopped fine
½ cup orange peel, graded
½ cup lemon peel, grated
4 cloves garlic, minced

Wash and dry poultry. On a clean surface, gently rub salt (and additional brine ingredients, if desired) into the surface area of the chicken, making sure to get brine under skin flaps, crevices, and joint fold areas.

Place poultry into a gallon-size food grade plastic bag or a large airtight container. Pour any remaining dry brine over chicken. Refrigerate chicken for 1 day. Remove from refrigerator and rub the brine that has accumulated into the poultry. Return to the refrigerator for 12 hours. Repeat process every 12 hours for the next 36 hours.

Remove chicken from storage, discard bag or wash container. Pat chicken dry. Store in refrigerator for up to 2 days, freezer pack, or cook chicken per normal methods.

GUINNESS BEER CAN CHICKEN

The process sounds and looks a little ridiculous, but the results are amazing! I particularly love using a dark, rich beer like Guinness as it adds complex flavor, but, if you prefer a lighter brew, any of your favorite beers may be substituted. Each will give the chicken a subtly different taste, but all will deliver great results.

Ingredients:
1 whole chicken
1 can of Guinness stout
2 Tbsp. olive oil
1 Tbsp. honey
1 Tbsp. fresh rosemary, chopped
1 clove garlic, minced
1 Tbsp. sea salt
1 tsp. mustard seed

In a small mixing bowl, add olive oil, honey, rosemary, garlic, sea salt, and mustard seed. Mix until fully combined.

Rinse and dry chicken. On a clean surface, rub chicken with oil mix, making sure to coat the inside, outside, and all folds.

Preheat barbecue grill. The recipe requires indirect heat for the best results. If you are using a charcoal grill, once charcoal is ready, push coals to outer rim of grill, leaving just a thin layer of coal in the center. If you are using a gas grill, once the grill has heated, turn off the center burners, leaving the outer burners on.

Open and empty about one-third of the beer can (a few good swigs will do!). Emptying the beer can slightly will keep it from boiling over. Place the beer can top side up on the grill. Place the chicken cavity-side down atop the beer can until the legs are balanced on the grill. The beer can will be inserted about halfway into the cavity of the bird. Close grill lid, and cook at a medium-high temperature for about 60 minutes or until the chicken is fully cooked to a safe temperature. Remove from grill. Using protective gloves or oven mitts, carefully remove chicken from beer can. Set beer can aside; discard when cooled. Transfer chicken to platter, slice, quarter or piece, and serve.

DRYING—NO SUNSCREEN NEEDED!

Dehydrating foods is one of the best ways to render them into portable preserves ideal for snacking, hiking, camping, and other on-the-go adventures. The downside to dehydrating is that it removes the most nutrients from raw foods. However, it does not remove other beneficial properties such as fiber, and it keeps the food in a natural state without any need for chemicals, salts, or sugars. Dried snacks are far superior to preprocessed fried, high sodium, or sugar-laden foods.

WHAT SHALL I DRY?

Bread, pasta, herbs, fruit, vegetables, nuts, and flowers are all excellent choices for drying. In addition to being preserved in their natural state, they may be formed into chips, crackers, breadsticks, jerky, granola bars, and—my favorite—fruit leather, which is an excellent way to utilize your overripe fruits.

HOW SHALL I DRY IT?

Three standard methods exist for dehydrating foods: sun, oven, and specialized dehydrator appliances. Each has advantages and disadvantages. Use the following chart to help you select the method that's right for you.

Sun Drying	Oven Drying	Dehydrator Drying
Low-cost materials	Low-cost materials (assuming oven is already owned)	Range in price from $49 to $500
Natural	Requires large amounts of electricity or gas	Requires electricity, generally low voltage
Outdoor conditions must be dry and hot with low humidity	Needs constant attention	Requires little attention
Temperature needs to be 85 degrees Celsius or higher	Drying temperature may be inconsistent	Drying temperature is regulated
Air provides adequate circulation	Low air circulation can cause problems	Air circulation is regulated at optimum levels
Food must be brought in at night and during storms	Oven door must be kept open	Food can be scheduled to dry overnight
Bugs, dust, and traffic pollution can be an issue	You will not be able to use stove for cooking or baking during drying time	Compact design can be set up on tabletop or countertop
May take 3–5 days	May take up to 20 hours	May take up to 16 hours
Highest risk of mold	Highest risk of burning foods	Lowest risk of burning and mold
Best for users who live in dry, hot, low-humidity climates or who are highly energy conscious	Best for beginners who are testing drying for the first time or for users with low-volume drying needs	Best for users who have high-volume drying needs

Herbs are the exception to conventional drying methods as they can be easily air dried within the home. Simply bundle the herbs in small bunches and tie with a string, then hang leaf side down in a warm, dark area with good air circulation until fully dried. If you are drying leaves, lay them flat on a mesh screen and allow them to dry in a warm, dry area with good air circulation. Once herbs are fully dried, they can be stored whole or ground in an air-tight container for use in recipes or teas.

Horseradish and ginger root are better frozen than dried. Ginger root should be stored in a freezer-safe bag. When needed, simply remove and grate the desired amount, then return ginger root to bag and refreeze for up to one year. Horseradish should be grated and stored in an airtight freezer container. When needed, scoop out portion required for recipe, reseal container and return to freezer for up to one year.

Dried goods may be stored in an airtight container in a cool, dark, dry place for up to two months. Ideally, containers should not be clear, as light will degrade dried foods. If produce is completely dehydrated to a brittle state, storage time may be increased to up to four months. Dehydrated foods may be frozen to extend storage time, but must be promptly used after defrosting.

BASIC FRUIT LEATHER RECIPE

Fruit leather is a perfect choice for using overripened fruits. Remove peels, cores, seeds, bruises, and signs of disease or insect damage. Chop fruit and puree in a food processor. Once you have 2 cups of pureed fruit, mix with 1 tsp. lemon juice. If preferred, for seeded fruits such as strawberries and raspberries, strain with a sieve to de-seed.

For sun or stove drying, line a baking tray with a food-grade silicone sheet or parchment paper for baking. Pour puree in an even layer across the sheet, to approximately a ¼-inch thickness.

Dry in oven at 120 degrees Fahrenheit for 6–8 hours.

Sun dry, preferably on a hot (80 degrees or higher) day with low humidity for 8–12 hours.

Dry in dehydrator per manufacturer's instructions for your dehydrator model.

When fruit leather is dried to "leather" consistency, cut into squares or strips. Store in an airtight container, using wax paper between layers to prevent sticking. Container may be stored in a cool, dark, dry space for up to 2 months.

Alternatively, to help prevent fruit leather pieces from sticking together, the pieces may be dust coated with powdered oats, ground cinnamon, ground nutmeg, or pumpkin pie spice. In a large bowl, add 1 cup of preferred coating. Add a few fruit leather pieces (squares work best) to the bowl. Gently toss until pieces are lightly coated. Remove and continue process until all fruit leather is lightly coated. Store fruit in airtight container in a cool, dark, dry space. Discard (compost) remaining coating.

It's fun to add toppings such as chopped nuts, diced raisins, coconut flakes, and flax seed. Sprinkle the toppings atop the fruit puree after it is spread out across the drying pan. The toppings will stick naturally during the drying process, but you may also gently press them in with a spatula or your fingertips.

Try one of my favorite fruit leather combinations or use them to inspire your own creations:

Ingredient 1 +	Ingredient 2 +	Ingredient 3
1 cup apple puree	1 cup pear puree	Dusted with oat powder
1 cup apple puree	½ cup strawberry puree	½ cup raspberry puree
1 cup strawberry puree	½ cup blueberry puree	½ cup raspberry puree
1 cup pear puree	½ cup blueberry puree	½ cup raspberry puree
1 cup pear puree	1 cup blackberry puree	Topped with flax seed
1 cup peach puree	1 cup apricot puree	Dusted with cinnamon
1 cup peach puree	1 cup raspberry puree	Topped with chopped walnuts
1 cup grape puree	1 cup blackberry puree	Topped with chopped pecans
1 cup rhubarb puree	1 cup cherry puree	Dusted with oat powder
1 cup peach puree	1 cup mango puree	Topped with coconut flakes
1 cup apple puree	1 cup peach puree	Dusted with nutmeg
2 cups strawberry puree	Topped with diced dried cranberries	Dusted with oat powder

 Chick Tip: When drying fruit leather (or any produce or meat) be sure to ensure every piece is completely dry throughout to prevent spoilage. Also be sure to label jars clearly with the type of fruit leather and date processed.

POWDERED VEGETABLE SOUP MIX
Yield: 4-6 servings

Ingredients:
*½ cup sun-dried tomatoes,
    ground*
¼ cup dried carrots, ground
¼ cup dried green beans, ground
½ cup lentils, dried
1 cup dried pasta shells
1 Tbsp. onion, dried and chopped
1 tsp. parsley, ground
1 tsp. rosemary, ground
1 tsp. oregano, ground
1 tsp. garlic powder

Layer or mix all ingredients in an airtight storage bag or container. Store in a cool, dark and dry place for up to 2 months.

When ready to use, in a medium saucepan over medium heat, add 4 cups of water and soup mix. Stir until fully combined. Increase heat to medium-high and bring to a boil for 1 minute. Reduce heat and simmer for 45 minutes, stirring occasionally.

A PRESCRIPTION FOR YOUR CURE

Keeping a journal of preservation is a terrific way to keep track of what methods of preservation worked best with your harvest. It also provides a quick reference of the amounts and types of food you have in storage and will help you make plans for next year's harvest.

Handy information to track in your journal:

- Number of chickens butchered
- Pounds of meat obtained
- Methods by which meat was preserved
- Number of hens in your coop
- Egg yield per week
- Methods by which eggs were preserved
- Types of plants in garden
- Number of seeds planted for each plant variety
- Yield by crop
- Quantity of crop preserved
- Methods by which crops were preserved
- Dates of preservation
- Quantity of preserved goods by type
- Date preserved goods were used up
- Date preserved goods were gifted
- Quantity gifted
- Observations
- Lessons learned
- Ideas

When you have finished preserving your bounty, keep your journal in an easy-to-access location to inventory your goods and mark off what has been used.

Prior to the planting season or prior to raising new baby chicks, use your journal to help you determine your needs. Did you run out of an item quickly? You may need to plant more seeds or raise more chickens during the next season. Do you have an excess of a particular crop? It's time to scale back during the next growing season.

Ultimately, a well-kept journal will be your constant go-to resource for perfecting your food and preservation plans.

6. Get Fried:
Dishing Up Poultry and Eggs in the Kitchen

You've raised your chicks, harvested and stored all of your produce. Now it's time to create culinary masterpieces from your organic bounty. In traditional farm-to-table cooking, meals are prepared in the spirit of highlighting the true flavors and essence of every ingredient used. Each dish has a focal point, and each bite takes you back to the garden or sun-drenched field.

As we began our sustainable journey with chickens, it only seems fitting that we begin our journey in the kitchen the same way.

Name That Chicken. Test your kitchen chicken IQ by seeing if you can match up these common terms with the definition. Hint: Some terms have the same answer!

1. Broiler	a. Three- to five-month-old chicken, weighing around five to seven pounds, typically roasted whole
2. Fryer	b. An unsexed male chicken about eighteen months old, with large portions of light meat, typically roasted
3. Roaster	
4. Baking Hen	c. Older male chicken with tough dark meat, typically slow-roasted or used for stew
5. Stewing Hens	d. A young chicken, around two months old, weighing around two to four pounds, suitable for all types of cooking
6. Rooster	
7. Capon	e. A small broiler chicken, weighing around one to two pounds, typically roasted whole
8. Cornish Hen	f. Older hen with tougher meat, typically slow roasted or used for stew

Answer Key: 1.d, 2.d, 3.a, 4.f, 5.f, 6.c, 7.b, 8.e

WHAT COLOR IS MY CHICKEN?

From the time it is butchered and processed to when it's cooked and plated, the color of chicken can vary dramatically. The breed, age, diet, and storage method will all influence color and appearance of the meat. Familiarizing yourself with the color will help you address imperfections like freezer burn and recognize signs of spoilage.

WHITE—A bluish-white is perfectly normal for fresh chicken. Excessive white, hard spots are most likely found on freezer-stored chicken and are a sign of freezer burn. Simply trim the white spots prior to eating. A white cast to the meat is common after cooking, particularly after boiling the chicken.

BLUE—Blue hues are an indicator of lean meat and most commonly found in meat from young birds.

YELLOW—Higher fat content in the skin or a diet that includes marigolds may cause a bright yellow skin and flesh. This is a common color found in fresh or processed chicken.

RED—Older chickens may have an excess of protein in their cells that produces a reddish hue.

PINK—A well-exercised chicken muscle will have a pinkish hue. Common color to see in chicken legs and thighs. Pink hues after cooking to proper temperatures are normal, especially closer to the bone of the chicken. Smoking a chicken will typically result in a strong pink cast to the meat.

Ground chicken will generally be light pink in color if more white meat or skin was used in processing, or dark pink in color if more dark meat was used in processing.

TAN—Common color after cooking, particularly if the chicken is grilled, roasted, or sautéed/browned.

GREEN—A green color is most commonly found in the chicken liver. The giblets (heart, liver, and gizzard) typically range from dark brown to yellow in color. If the liver is green, it's an indicator of excessive bile in the liver from the gallbladder. While considered by many to be safe for consumption, it's generally discarded.

GRAY—A gray tint is generally caused by chicken coming into contact with air due to insufficient or faulty packaging. Gray may also be a sign of freezer burn in chicken that has been processed for freezer storage. Most importantly, though, gray can be a sign of spoilage.

FADED or DARK—All of the above colors may fade or darken in hue with proper storage and cooking methods. It's considered a normal occurrence.

Chick Tip: If the chicken meat is gray, exhibits a foul odor, or is excessively slimy or sticky to the touch, proceed with extreme caution. These are all considered signs of spoiled chicken that will not be safe for consumption.

CAN I MICROWAVE CHICKEN?

Microwaving is not the preferred method, but microwaving chicken is certainly a modern, viable alternative for cooking. As with every method, microwaved chicken needs to reach a safe internal temperature of at least 165 degrees Fahrenheit.

Approximate cooking times, using a standard setting microwave setting are:

Whole Chicken	9 minutes per pound
Chicken Parts, Bone-In	7 minutes per pound
Boneless Chicken	6 minutes per pound
Cornish Hens	8 minutes per pound

Note: Microwave temperatures may vary and it may be helpful to reduce power to achieve the best results. You may need to experiment a little to achieve the best results.

Whole chickens or Cornish hens are best cooked without stuffing using a microwave-safe casserole dish. Boneless chicken and chicken parts may be spread out and cooked on a microwave-safe dish or by using a microwave steamer.

HANDY KITCHEN CHARTS

Even with the best of intentions, there will come a time when you are missing a key ingredient for a recipe. Rather than expending time and energy to race to the store, keep this recipe swap-chart nearby to handle the emergency.

Do note that substituting ingredients may alter the flavor, consistency, and end result of a recipe, but when you are in a pinch or need to make a swap due to dietary concerns, it's certainly a blessing to have an alternative!

Common Ingredient Substitutes	
IF YOU RUN OUT OF...	**SUBSTITUTE WITH...**
1 egg (for baking)	2 egg yolks
1 Tbsp. butter (for sautéing)	1 Tbsp. olive oil
1 Tbsp. butter (for baking)	1 Tbsp. shortening
1 square of baking chocolate	3 Tbsp. powdered cocoa plus 1 Tbsp. butter (or shortening)
1 cup buttermilk	1 cup milk mixed with 1 Tbsp. of vinegar (or lemon juice)
1 cup milk	½ cup evaporated milk plus ½ cups water
1 Tbsp. flour (for thickening)	½ Tbsp. cornstarch
1 tsp. baking powder	¼ tsp. baking soda plus ½ tsp. cream of tartar
1 cup self-rising flour (for baking)	1 cup all-purpose flour and omit baking powder and salt from recipe
1 cup all-purpose flour (for baking)	1 cup of sorghum flour, 1 cup of wheat flour, 1 cup of oat flour, 1 cup of buckwheat flour, or 1 cup of quinoa
1 Tbsp. fresh herbs	1 tsp. dried herbs

IF YOU RUN OUT OF...	SUBSTITUTE WITH...
1 cup sugar	¾ cup honey
2 Tbsp. olive oil (for sautéing)	2 Tbsp. canola oil, 2 Tbsp. vegetable oil, 2 Tbsp. of coconut oil, 2 Tbsp. peanut oil, 2 Tbsp. sesame oil or 2 Tbsp. grapeseed oil
1 cup vegetable oil (for baking)	1 cup canola oil, 1 cup olive oil, or 1 cup of applesauce
1 cup vegetable oil (for frying)	1 cup canola oil, 1 cup peanut oil
1 Tbsp. basil	1 Tbsp. mint
1 Tbsp. allspice	¼ Tbsp. ground cloves
1 Tbsp. cinnamon	½ Tbsp. allspice
1 Tbsp. mustard	1 tsp. mustard powder
1 cup honey	1 cup of maple syrup
1 cup beer	1 cup unsweetened apple juice
1 cup cream cheese	1 cup plain Greek yogurt
1 tsp. lemon juice	1 tsp. white vinegar
1 cup sugar	1 cup brown sugar, ¾ cup honey
1 cup white wine	1 cup chicken stock, 1 cup white grape juice plus 1 tsp. vinegar
1 cup red wine	1 cup unsweetened grape juice
1 cup sour cream	1 cup plain yogurt

RECIPE MEASUREMENT EQUIVALENCY CHEAT SHEET

No matter how much time you've spent in the kitchen, there's still that day when you will sit and ponder over how many teaspoons are in a tablespoon because you forgot the tablespoon set is in the dishwasher. Or you'll find a fabulous recipe you love, only to find the measurements are in cups and you need milliliters. For any scenario of measurement doubt, we've got you covered with this handy chart.

CUP	TBSP	TSP	FLUID OUNCE	MILLILITER
1 cup	16 Tbsp.	48 tsp.	8 oz.	237 ml
¾ cup	12 Tbsp.	36 tsp.	6 oz.	177 ml
⅔ cup	11 Tbsp.	32 tsp.	5 oz.	158 ml
½ cup	8 Tbsp.	24 tsp.	4 oz.	118 ml
⅓ cup	5 Tbsp.	16 tsp.	3 oz.	79 ml
¼ cup	4 Tbsp.	12 tsp.	2 oz.	59 ml
⅛ cup	2 Tbsp.	6 tsp.	1 oz.	30 ml
1⁄16 C	1 Tbsp.	3 tsp.	.5 oz.	15 ml

Want to be amazingly clever in a fun DIY way? Photocopy this chart and découpage onto a recycled piece of heavy cardboard, then attach a few magnets to the back, and voilà! Instant measurement magnet to stick to your favorite metal appliance.

PLAY WITH YOUR FOOD SAFELY

Not many people like to think or talk about the icky side of the kitchen—the deep, dark, invisible places where germs reside. But things like salmonella are real threats to your culinary enjoyment. The good news is, with a few good habits, you can dramatically reduce or eliminate the threat of most foodborne illnesses. Trust me, your tummy (and your family and friends) will thank you for the extra precautionary measures!

DO gently buff or wash all eggs as soon as they are brought into the home and wash your hands thoroughly after. There's some debate about whether farm eggs need to be washed, but, as the saying goes, "sorry" is not where you want to wind up.

DO cook eggs and poultry (and other meats) to the proper internal temperature. Current food safety standards for eggs is 160 degrees Fahrenheit and for chicken 165 degrees Fahrenheit. Always check FoodSafety.gov for temperature safety standards.

DON'T cross-contaminate foods. Raw meat and veggies do not play well together. Wash your hands, utensils, equipment, and work surfaces before and after handing each food item.

DO use a quality cutting board with antibacterial properties. Marble, glass, and wood are all excellent choices. Be sure to clean it properly after use, according to the material's needs.

DON'T use eggs with broken shells. If they are cracked or leaking, compost them! Dig a small hole in your compost bin and crack the egg into it, crumble up the eggshells, then bury to help avoid odor problems.

DO store your foods at proper temperatures. Bacteria multiplies rapidly between temperatures of 40 degrees Fahrenheit and 140 degrees Fahrenheit. If cold or hot foods will be set out for a long time (such as for buffet use or holiday gatherings), use ice or cold packs to keep your cold items fresh and use food warmers for hot foods.

DO use a meat thermometer to test proper temperatures for chicken and a standard instant-read thermometer for other foods. It is the most accurate way to test for doneness.

DON'T consider cooking times in recipes to be 100 percent accurate. Always check temperatures when pertinent, and look for signs of doneness—for example, the browning of crust on bread.

DON'T trust that your oven temperature is accurate. Invest in an oven thermometer to monitor the internal temperature of your oven, and make adjustments to ensure proper temperature for recipes, when necessary.

DO read recipes thoroughly to ensure you understand and follow the steps properly. If you experience recipe failure, it is often due to missing an important step.

A DOZEN FRESH WAYS TO PREPARE YOUR EGGS

Soft, over-easy, scrambled, poached—no matter how you take your eggs, you'll often find yourself with an abundance from your well-tended flock. If you limit yourself to using the extras solely for baking, you'll be missing out on a wealth of egg delights. This versatile, protein-packed oval gem is the base for many a tasty dish. Try one of these recipe ideas and you may find yourself saying sayonara to scrambled.

FRESH GARDEN FRITTATA

Yield: Serves 4

Ingredients:

10 eggs
1 onion, chopped
1 red pepper, chopped
2 cloves garlic, chopped
1 tomato, seeded and chopped
1 cup sharp cheddar cheese,
*   shredded*
2 Tbsp. parsley, chopped
2 Tbsp. olive oil
Salt and pepper (optional)

Preheat oven to 400 degrees Fahrenheit.

In a large mixing bowl, add eggs and lightly beat until smooth. Set aside.

In a large cast iron skillet, heat butter over medium heat until it foams. Add onion, garlic, and red pepper. Add a pinch of salt and pepper. Sauté until tender. Add tomato and parsley. Pour eggs over mixture. Sprinkle cheese on top of egg mix. Cook 3 minutes (or until eggs are starting to set).

Remove skillet from stovetop. Place skillet in oven for 10–12 minutes (frittata should be puffed). Remove from oven and serve immediately.

 Chick Tip: Fresh eggs are not ideal for hard-boiling as they are difficult to peel. When making hard-cooked eggs, opt to use last week's dozen.

SCOTCH CHICKEN EGGS

Yield: Serves 8

Ingredients:
8 eggs, hard-boiled and peeled
4 eggs, lightly beaten
2 lbs. chicken, ground
1 cup all-purpose flour
4 cups Brown Bread Crumbs
  (page 201)

Preheat oven to 350 degrees Fahrenheit.

Divide the ground chicken into eight equal portions and flatten into patty shapes. Place a hard-boiled egg in the center of each patty. Gently mold the patty around the egg until it forms a completely sealed outer layer.

Lightly flour the ground chicken layer (roll oval ball shape in flour). Coat the floured ball with beaten egg, then roll in bread crumbs, covering evenly.

Place breaded egg patties on a greased cookie sheet, leaving a 1-inch space between them. Bake for 45–50 minutes. Remove from oven, cool for 5 minutes. Slice in half and serve. Scotch Chicken Eggs are terrific served over a fresh bed of lettuce leaves with a sliced tomato. They are also quite good with Hollandaise sauce.

EASY HOLLANDAISE SAUCE

Yield: 1 cup

Ingredients:
3 egg yolks
½ cup butter, cut into four equal
  pats
1 Tbsp. lemon juice

Using a double boiler, heat water in bottom tier until hot, but not boiling.

In a small bowl, whisk egg yolks and lemon juice until frothy. Add egg mixture to top-tier pan of the double boiler; continue to whisk. Add one pat of butter, stirring continuously until butter is melted. Repeat with the remaining three pats of butter. Continue stirring until all butter is melted and sauce is thickened. Remove from heat, pour over Scotch Chicken Eggs (see above) or other dishes, as desired.

ITALIAN POACHED EGGS
Yield: Serves 4

Ingredients:

4 eggs

2 Roma tomatoes, sliced

4 Tbsp. basil, chopped

4 cups fresh spinach leaves

4 Tbsp. balsamic vinegar

2 tsp. olive oil

Using four small serving plates, layer 1 cup of spinach on each plate. Add a layer of sliced Roma tomato to each plate.

Poach eggs according to preference. Layer poached egg on top of tomato. Sprinkle 1 Tbsp. basil over each egg. Drizzle 1 Tbsp. balsamic vinegar and ½ tsp. olive oil over each egg. Serve immediately.

Chick Tip: Want fresh eggs for breakfast but in a hurry? Grab a coffee mug and microwave a tasty scramble in less than 2 minutes! Add 2 eggs, 2 Tbsp. milk, and 2 Tbsp. sharp cheddar cheese (shredded) to the mug, and whisk until frothy. Microwave on high for 30 seconds, stir. Microwave for an additional 45 seconds and enjoy your egg breakfast on the go.

BROWN BREAD BREAKFAST SOUFFLÉ

Yield: Serves 6–8

Ingredients:

8 eggs

1 loaf day-old Brown Bread
  (page 200)

8 ounces cream cheese, softened

1 ½ cups milk

½ cup pure maple syrup

½ cup half-and-half

½ tsp. Vanilla Extract (page 115)

Lightly coat a 9 x 13-inch baking pan lightly with butter.

In a large mixing bowl, beat cream cheese until smooth. Add eggs one by one, mixing each until fully incorporated before adding the next. Add milk, half and half, maple syrup, and vanilla; mix until smooth. Set mix aside.

Slice brown bread into 1-inch slices. Cut brown bread slices into approximately 1-inch cubes until entire loaf is cubed. Add cubed bread to the baking dish, spread in an even layer. Pour cream cheese mixture over the top of the bread, evenly covering the bread. (If there are any bread pieces that do not get covered by the cream cheese mixture, use a fork to press them into the mix until they have a light coating.)

Cover baking pan and refrigerate overnight (minimum of 8 hours). After mix has rested from 8 or more hours, remove bread mixture from refrigerator and uncover.

Preheat oven to 375 degrees Fahrenheit.

Bake for 45–50 minutes. Remove and allow to cool for 10 minutes. Cut and serve immediately with maple syrup. Optionally, cinnamon or powdered sugar may be sprinkled atop soufflé prior to serving.

TEX-MEX EGG BURRITOS

Yield: Serves 4

Ingredients:
4 eggs
½ cup pepper-jack cheese,
shredded
2 scallions, minced
1 Tbsp. canola oil
4 whole wheat tortillas
Tomatillo Tart Salsa (page 112)

In a medium cast iron skillet, heat oil over medium-high heat. Reduce heat to low. Fry eggs over a low heat, cooking until the eggs are set. Remove from skillet; set aside.

Warm tortillas in skillet over medium heat, 1 minute per side.

Place warm tortillas on individual serving plates. Layer with egg. Sprinkle one quarter of scallions over each egg. Sprinkle 1 ounce of cheese over each egg. Add a thin layer of salsa. Roll tortillas, serve immediately.

SPRING EGG SALAD

Yield: Serves 4

Ingredients:
6 eggs, hard-boiled and chopped
6 cups spring lettuce leaves (any)
6 spring onions, chopped
½ cup olive oil
2 tsp. vinegar
1 tsp. Dijon mustard
¼ tsp. sugar

In a small mixing bowl, combine olive oil, vinegar, mustard, and sugar to create a vinaigrette.

In a large salad bowl, add lettuce, eggs, and onions. Pour vinaigrette over salad. Toss lightly, serve immediately. Brown bread (page 200) is an excellent accompaniment to this dish.

Chick Tip: Spring egg salad is even more fabulous when the hard-boiled eggs are still slightly warm when prepping. To prepare directly after hard-boiling, immerse eggs in a bowl of ice water for 3 minutes, then remove eggs and proceed to peel the shells.

SUN-SPECKLED PEPPER EGGS

Yield: Serves 2

Ingredients:

4 eggs

1 large yellow bell pepper (a green, red, or orange bell pepper may be substituted)

1 Tbsp. olive oil

Salt and pepper

Slice pepper horizontally into 1-inch slices. Remove seeds. (Reserve the ends of the pepper for seasoning salads or dinner dishes later.)

Heat oil in a medium cast iron skillet over a medium flame. Reduce heat to medium-low. Arrange 4 pepper ring slices on the bottom the pan. Gently crack one egg into the center of each pepper ring slice. The pepper ring will form a "wall" around the egg, allowing it to cook in the center. Sprinkle the top of each egg with a little salt and pepper.

Cover pan and cook for 6–8 minutes (egg whites should be fully set). Remove and serve immediately.

BIRDS IN A BROWN BREAD NEST

Yield: Serves 4

Ingredients:

4 eggs

4 slices of Brown Bread (page 200)

1 clove garlic, diced

2 Tbsp. olive oil

½ cup Parmigiano-Reggiano, shredded

Cut a hole (1-inch diameter) in the center of each slice of brown bread.

Heat oil in a medium cast iron skillet over a medium flame. Add garlic and sauté until tender. Arrange bread in a flat layer in the skillet. Fry 2–3 minutes (bread should be lightly browned), then flip bread to other side. Gently crack one egg into the center of each bread slice.

Cover pan and cook for 2 minutes. Remove cover. Flip the bread and cook for 1 minute. Flip bread again (top side of egg should be facing up), sprinkle cheese over bread and egg slices. Cook for 1 minute. Remove bread with egg center from the pan, serve immediately.

FORAGED FRIED EGGS WITH SAGE BUTTER

Yield: Serves 4

Ingredients:

4 eggs

1 cup morel mushrooms (may substitute baby bella mushrooms)

6 cups collard greens (may substitute kale)

2 cloves of garlic, sliced

2 Tbsp. olive oil

4 Tbsp. butter

1 Tbsp. fresh sage, diced

Heat butter in a medium iron skillet over medium heat until frothy. Add sage and sauté for 2 minutes. Remove from heat; set aside.

Heat oil in a large cast iron skillet over high heat. Add mushrooms and sauté until tender (about 5 minutes). Reduce heat to medium. Add garlic and greens, sauté for 1 minute. Add 2 Tbsp. of water. Sauté until garlic is soft and greens are wilted.

Push greens to the side of the skillet. Gently crack eggs into center of skillet. Cook for 4 minutes. Remove eggs and greens from heat. Set 4 breakfast plates. Layer one-fourth of the greens on each plate. Place one-fourth of eggs (keeping yolks intact) atop each bed of greens. Drizzle with sage butter. Serve immediately.

EASY CHEESY SOUFFLÉ

Yield: Serves 4-6

Ingredients:

6 eggs

1 cup milk

¼ cup sharp cheddar cheese, grated

¼ cup Swiss cheese, grated

1 tsp. fresh parsley, chopped fine

1 Tbsp. butter

Preheat oven to 450 degrees Fahrenheit.

Heat butter and milk in a small saucepan over medium heat, stir until butter is fully melted and milk is warm. Remove from heat.

In a medium mixing bowl, add eggs; whip until frothy. Add warm milk, cheese and parsley. Stir until fully mixed. Pour mix into a 9 x 13-inch glass baking pan. Bake for 20 minutes or until eggs are fully set.

Remove from oven, and serve immediately.

SCALLOPED EGGS

Yield: Serves 4-6

This tasty dish makes great use of leftover baked potatoes.

Ingredients:

4 eggs, hard-boiled and sliced
    thin
2 potatoes, baked, cooled and
    sliced thin
1 cup milk
1 cup Brown Bread Crumbs
    (page 201)
1 Tbsp. butter
1 Tbsp. flour
1 Tbsp. fresh parsley, chopped
    fine
Salt and pepper

Preheat oven to 375 degrees Fahrenheit.

In a small saucepan over medium heat, add milk, butter, and flour. Stir gently until warmed and slightly thickened. Remove from heat, set aside.

In a greased 9 x 13-inch glass baking dish, add a layer of sliced potatoes. Top with a layer of sliced egg. Add a layer of sliced potatoes and then another layer of egg. If you have any leftover eggs and potatoes, spread out evenly across the top layer.

Pour milk sauce evenly over potatoes and eggs. Sprinkle a pinch of salt and a pinch of pepper across the top. Sprinkle breadcrumbs in an even layer across the top. Bake for 25 minutes. Remove from oven, cool for 5 minutes, and serve.

THE CHICKEN CAME FIRST IN THESE FOURTEEN DISHES

Fried chicken is notably the most popular chicken dish, followed quickly by baked, roasted, and grilled. No matter how you prepare it, chicken is a versatile meat. Want a quick change of chicken? From my kitchen to yours, here are fourteen of my favorite crowd-pleasing recipes.

SUMMER SKILLET STEW

Yield: Serves 4

Ingredients:

3 lbs. chicken parts (dark or
*   white, excluding wings)*
3 cups whole tomatoes, peeled
1 eggplant
1 zucchini, diced
1 bell pepper, diced
2 Tbsp. fresh rosemary, chopped
2 Tbsp. fresh basil, chopped
2 Tbsp. fresh parsley, chopped
2 Tbsp. olive oil
Romano cheese, grated

Peel eggplant and chop (½-inch pieces). Drain tomatoes (if needed) and slice (½-inch thick). Wash chicken parts and pat dry.

Heat oil in a large cast iron skillet over medium heat. Add chicken parts; cook 5 minutes. Flip chicken parts and cook for an additional 5 minutes. Remove from pan.

Add eggplant, zucchini, and pepper. Cook 5 minutes (eggplant and zucchini should be soft). Add tomatoes. Add chicken (bone side down, skin side up), pushing vegetables aside to surround the chicken parts. Sprinkle rosemary, sage, and parsley on top of the stew.

Cover skillet and cook for 10 minutes. Reduce heat to low. Cook for 30–40 minutes (test internal temperature of chicken to determine readiness). Remove from heat.

Remove chicken from stew. Remove any skin or bones. Shred chicken.

Pour cooked vegetables into a large bowl. Add chicken. Gently stir until chicken is incorporated. Ladle stew into serving bowls. Top with shredded Romano and serve immediately.

PESTO CHICKEN

Yield: Serves 4

Ingredients:

*2 lbs. boneless, skinless chicken
   breast, diced*
8 oz. bowtie pasta
¾ cup pesto
¼ cup sun-dried tomatoes
¼ cup olive oil
Parmesan cheese, grated

Cook pasta (to al dente). Drain and set aside.

Heat 2 Tbsp. olive oil in a large cast iron skillet over medium-hot heat. Add chicken. Sauté until chicken is fully cooked. Add remaining olive oil and sun-dried tomatoes. Sauté for 5–6 minutes (until tomatoes are soft and heated). Remove from heat.

In a large mixing bowl, add pasta and pesto. Pour chicken and sun-dried tomatoes over the pasta. Gently toss until fully mixed. (If sauce is too thick, additional olive oil may be added.) Plate portions, top with Parmesan cheese, and serve immediately.

GARDEN CHICKEN CACCIATORE

Yield: Serves 4

Ingredients:

1 whole chicken
2 cups tomatoes, diced
1 cup white button mushrooms,
   diced
1 cup onion, chopped
1 green bell pepper, chopped
1 red bell pepper, chopped
4 cloves garlic, minced
1 cup flour
½ cup dry white wine
¼ cup butter
1 Tbsp. fresh parsley, chopped
1 tsp. fresh basil, chopped
1 tsp. fresh oregano, chopped
Preferred choice of pasta or rice,
   cooked

Cut chicken into pieces. Wash and pat dry. Lightly coat chicken pieces with flour.

Preheat oven to 350 degrees Fahrenheit.

Heat butter in a large cast iron skillet over medium-hot heat until frothy. Add chicken and sauté, turning until lightly browned on all sides. Remove chicken from skillet and set aside.

Add pepper, garlic, onions and mushrooms to skillet. Sauté until all ingredients are soft. Add tomatoes, parsley, basil, oregano, and wine. Reduce heat to medium. Cover skillet and cook sauce for 5 minutes. Remove from heat.

In a 10 x 13-inch glass baking dish, place chicken in a single layer. Pour sauce evenly over chicken. Cover baking dish with foil. Bake for 1 hour. Remove from oven and serve over rice or pasta.

DUTCH OVEN CHICKEN NOODLE SOUP
Yield: Serves 6–8

Ingredients:

*2 lbs. boneless, skinless chicken
  breasts*
*6 cups Freezer Chicken Stock
  (page 95)*
4 cups water
2 carrots, chopped
2 parsnips, chopped
2 celery stalks, chopped
1 onion, chopped
1 Tbsp. fresh parsley, chopped
½ Tbsp. fresh thyme, chopped
2 Tbsp. olive oil
1 bag fine egg noodles (12 oz.)
Salt and pepper

Heat oil in a Dutch oven over medium heat. Add carrots, parsnips, celery, onion, and thyme. Add a dash of salt and pepper. Sauté until all ingredients are soft and slightly browned.

Add chicken, stock, and water. Increase heat to high, and bring to a rolling boil. Reduce heat to medium-low, simmer for 25 minutes. Remove chicken breasts from soup. Shred or cube. Return chicken to pot.

Add egg noodles and parsley. Simmer for 10 minutes, stirring occasionally. Remove from heat. Allow soup to cool for 10 minutes. Ladle into soup bowls and serve.

BLACK WALNUT BUTTERNUT CHICKEN
Yield: Serves 4

Ingredients:

4 boneless chicken breasts,
  chopped
1 butternut squash
2 cups tomatoes, diced
1 cup Freezer Chicken Stock
  (page 95)
1 cup water
5 cloves of garlic, sliced thin
2 onions, sliced thin
¼ cup lemon juice
½ tsp. honey
1 Tbsp. fresh parsley, chopped
1 Tbsp. fresh cilantro, chopped
½ tsp. cinnamon, ground
½ tsp. nutmeg, ground
½ tsp. cloves, ground
4 Tbsp. olive oil
½ cup black walnuts, chopped
  coarse
Salt and pepper

Heat 2 Tbsp. olive oil in a Dutch oven over medium-high heat. Add chicken, cinnamon, nutmeg, and cloves. Sauté chicken, turning until lightly browned on all sides. Remove chicken and set aside.

Reduce heat to medium. Add onions and sauté until soft. Add garlic; sauté until garlic is soft. Add cilantro, parsley, tomatoes, water, and chicken stock. Stir gently for 1 minute. Add chicken. Cook 30 minutes.

While chicken is cooking, heat 2 Tbsp. olive oil in a medium skillet over medium heat. Add squash and honey. Sauté squash, turning until lightly browned on all sides. Remove from heat.

Add squash to chicken. Cook an additional 10–15 minutes (or until chicken is done). Reduce heat to low. Add lemon juice. Simmer for 5 minutes. Remove from heat. Plate, sprinkle with chopped black walnuts and serve immediately.

 Chick Tip: To cure over-salted soup, add a teaspoon of apple cider vinegar and a teaspoon of sugar to hot soup; mix in thoroughly.

SLOW COOKER WHITE BEAN CHILI

Yield: Serves 8

Ingredients:

1 lb. chicken, ground

1 onion, chopped

4 cloves of garlic, minced

*1 jalapeno pepper, seeded and
    diced*

*1 green bell pepper, seeded and
    diced*

*4 cups white beans (kidney
    or cannelloni, presoaked,
    rinsed, and drained)*

1 cup tomatoes, diced

*2 cups Freezer Chicken Stock
    (page 95)*

2 tsp. oregano, ground

1 tsp. cumin, ground

½ tsp. salt

½ tsp. pepper

In a medium cast iron skillet over medium heat, cook ground chicken until lightly browned. Remove from heat, drain grease and set aside.

Set large slow cooker to low for an 8-hour cook setting. Add all ingredients. Stir gently to fully mix. Set cover on slow cooker and allow to cook for 8-hour period.

After cooking time is complete, open lid on slow cooker, gently stir chili, then ladle into soup bowls for serving. Chili may be topped with shredded cheddar cheese, sour cream, or other preferred toppings.

 Chick Tip: If you don't have a meat grinder, chicken can be quickly ground using a food processor. Simply cut chicken into cubes, put in the food processor and pulse until ground.

WHOLE HONEY-GLAZED CHICKEN AND BROWN BREAD STUFFING

Yield: Serves 4

Ingredients:

*1 whole chicken, gutted, cleaned,
    and patted dry*
*4 cups day-old Brown Bread
    (page 200), cubed*
½ cup butter, melted
1 Tbsp. butter
1 small onion, diced
2 stalks of celery, chopped
½ cup dried apples, chopped
½ cups water
1 Tbsp. honey
½ tsp. cinnamon, ground
½ tsp. nutmeg, ground
½ tsp. cloves, ground

Preheat oven to 350 degrees Fahrenheit.

Heat 1 Tbsp. butter in a large cast iron skillet over medium heat until frothy. Add onion and celery, sauté until soft. Add bread, apple, water, cinnamon, nutmeg, and cloves. Stir gently to combine. Cover skillet and cook for 2 minutes. Remove stuffing from heat, set aside.

Stuff chicken cavity loosely with stuffing. Tuck wings and drumsticks in, gently tie with string or use cooking pins to secure.

In a small bowl, mix melted butter and honey. Place stuffed chicken on rack in roasting pan, breast side up. Brush honey butter mixture over the outside of the chicken, coating all exposed areas evenly.

Bake, uncovered for 1½ hours or until chicken is done and stuffing reaches an internal temperature of 165 degrees Fahrenheit. Baste every half hour with juices from cooking.

Remove from oven when finished, let sit for 10 minutes. Remove stuffing from chicken cavity and place into a serving bowl. Quarter or piece chicken and place on platter. Serve along with preferred accompaniments such as steamed vegetables, baked sweet potatoes or salad.

SPICY CHICKEN QUESADILLAS
Yield: Serves 4

Ingredients:

4 chicken breasts, boneless and skinless
8 flour tortillas (12-inch)
1 cup Monterey cheese, shredded
1 cup cheddar cheese, shredded
1 cup onion, chopped
2 tomatoes, diced
1 lime, juiced
1 jalapeno pepper, seeded and diced
1 green bell pepper, seeded and diced
2 Tbsp. fresh cilantro, chopped
2 Tbsp. olive oil

In a small bowl, add tomatoes, ½ cup onion, cilantro, jalapeno, and lime juice. Mix gently to combine to create a fresh pico de gallo. Set aside.

Cut chicken breasts into strips. Heat oil in a large cast iron skillet over medium heat. Add chicken, sauté until fully cooked. Remove chicken and set aside.

Add green pepper and ½ cup onions, sauté until soft and lightly browned.

In a large bowl, add chicken, sautéed onions and peppers, and one half of the pico de gallo. Gently mix.

In a small bowl, mix cheddar and Monterey cheeses.

Heat a new (clean) large cast iron skillet over medium heat. Place one flour tortilla in skillet. Spread ¼ cup cheese evenly across tortilla. Spread ¼ chicken mixture over cheese. Layer one flour tortilla over chicken. Cook until bottom tortilla is lightly browned (cheese will be slightly melted). Flip quesadilla over and cook until cheese is fully melted. Remove quesadilla and repeat process until all are cooked. Cut quesadillas into fourths. Serve with remaining pico de gallo and other garnishes, as desired.

 Chick Tip: Splitting boneless chicken breasts will reduce your cooking time for recipes or on the grill. To split, lay the breast flat. Starting with the thickest part of the breast, slice horizontally with a chef's knife to create two equal pieces.

CAPRESE SALAD CHICKEN

Yield: Serves 4

Ingredients:

*4 chicken breasts, boneless and
   skinless*
2 cups cherry tomatoes
6 cloves garlic, sliced
½ cup dry white wine
2 Tbsp. olive oil
8 oz. buffalo mozzarella, cubed
¼ cup fresh basil, chopped
balsamic vinegar

Heat oil in a large cast iron skillet over medium heat. Add chicken; sauté until fully cooked. Remove from heat, drain any grease from skillet, and set chicken aside on a platter.

Using the same skillet, still over medium heat, add wine, tomatoes, and garlic. Sauté until sauce thickens (tomatoes will crack open). Remove from heat. Pour sauce over chicken. Sprinkle fresh basil and mozzarella cubes over chicken. Serve immediately.

AUTUMN DUTCH OVEN-ROASTED CHICKEN

Yield: Serves 4

Ingredients:

1 whole chicken, pieced
*2 cups sweet potatoes, peeled
   and sliced thin*
1 cup whole cranberry sauce
½ tsp. black pepper, ground
½ tsp. ginger, ground

Preheat oven to 375 degrees Fahrenheit.

In a small bowl, mix cranberry sauce, ginger, and pepper. In Dutch oven, add chicken parts. Top chicken with sliced sweet potatoes. Pour cranberry sauce over sweet potatoes. Bake uncovered for 1 hour or until chicken is thoroughly cooked. Remove from oven, plate and serve.

OLIVE-STUFFED CHICKEN
Yield: Serves 4–6

Stuffing olives in chicken is a wonderful Old World technique and one of my favorite go-to dishes for a dinner party. It's equally wonderful the next day cold, chopped, and served with mixed greens.

Ingredients:
1 whole chicken
1 cup green olives
1 cup dry white wine
1 Tbsp. fresh thyme, chopped fine
2 dried bay leaves
2 Tbsp. olive oil
Salt and pepper

Preheat oven to 350 degrees Fahrenheit.

In a small mixing bowl, crumble bay leaves. Add thyme and a dash of salt and pepper, mix gently. Rub skin of chicken with spice mix. Stuff chicken cavity with olives and truss (secure) chicken legs and wings.

Place chicken in roasting pan. Rub chicken with olive oil. Bake for 90 minutes or until skin is browned and chicken is thoroughly cooked. Every 30 minutes during baking, baste chicken with pan juices. Remove chicken from oven and place on serving tray.

In a small bowl, mix 1 cup of pan juices with wine. Slice chicken and plate. Drizzle wine sauce over chicken and serve.

WINTER CHICKEN SHEPHERD'S PIE
Yield: Serves 8

Traditional Shepherd's Pie, sometimes referred to as Cottage Pie, was known as a "poor man's dish" that made use of root vegetables and any meat that was available. Over time, beef and lamb have taken center stage for this dish. Chicken, however, is an excellent choice, providing a savory flavor profile and a refreshing change for this classic.

Ingredients:

4 lbs. chicken, boneless and skin-less, cubed
4 cups Chicken Stock (page 95)
4 cloves garlic, minced
1 Tbsp. ginger, minced
1 red onion, diced
3 lbs. potatoes
1 cup carrots, peeled and chopped
1 cup parsnips, peeled and chopped
1 cup milk
½ cup butter
4 bay leaves, whole
½ tsp. black peppercorn, ground
5 Tbsp. olive oil
Flour
Salt and pepper

Preheat oven to 325 degrees Fahrenheit.

Heat 2 Tbsp. oil in a Dutch oven over medium heat. While oil is heating, coat chicken lightly with flour. Add one half of chicken to Dutch oven. Sauté chicken, turning until lightly browned on all sides. Repeat with remaining half of chicken.

Add 1 Tbsp. oil, garlic and ginger to Dutch oven. Sauté over medium heat until soft. Add browned chicken. Add stock, onions, peppercorn, and bay leaves, and gently stir to mix ingredients. Cook until all ingredients are warmed, but stock is not boiling. Remove from heat, cover and transfer to oven. Bake for 2 hours.

While stew is baking, boil potatoes in one pot and carrots and parsnips in another until both are fork tender. Drain potatoes and carrot/parsnip mix. In a large bowl, add potatoes, carrots, parsnips, milk, and butter. Mash together until thoroughly incorporated.

After stew has baked for 2 hours, remove from oven and uncover. Remove bay leaves. Increase oven heat to 375 degrees Fahrenheit.

Top stew in Dutch oven evenly with mashed vegetables. Return to oven and bake uncovered for 45 minutes (top should be golden brown). Remove from oven, allow to cool for 10 minutes. Ladle equal portions of stew and root vegetables into bowls, and serve.

 Chick Tip: Though they each have their own flavor, parsnips and carrots are generally interchangeable in recipes. If the recipe calls for parsnips and you do not have any on hand, swap in carrots and vice versa.

EASY CHEESY GARLIC CHICKEN
Yield: Serves 4

Ingredients:
4 chicken breasts, boneless and
   skinless
2 cups tomatoes, diced
1 cup fresh mozzarella, grated
4 cloves of garlic, minced
2 Tbsp. fresh basil, chopped
1 Tbsp. fresh rosemary, chopped
1 Tbsp. fresh oregano, chopped

Preheat oven to 375 degrees Fahrenheit.

In a 10 x 13-inch glass baking dish, add tomatoes, garlic, basil, rosemary, and oregano. Stir gently to mix. Place chicken breasts on top of tomato mix. Bake for 35–40 minutes (or until chicken is done). Remove from oven.

Use a spoon to ladle and cover tops of chicken breasts with tomatoes. Sprinkle cheese evenly over chicken breasts. Return baking dish to oven. Bake for 5–10 minutes (or until cheese is bubbly). Remove from oven; serve immediately with rice or pasta.

CREAMY CHICKEN BAKE

Yield: Serves 4

Ingredients:

*4 chicken breasts or 8 chicken
thighs, boneless and skinless*
*1 cup Freezer Chicken Stock
(page 95)*
1 cup light cream
1 cup baby carrots, chopped
1 cup peas, shelled
2 cloves of garlic, minced
2 Tbsp. fresh parsley, chopped
½ tsp. black pepper, ground
½ tsp. salt

Preheat oven to 375 degrees Fahrenheit.

Rub chicken pieces with salt and pepper. Set aside.

In a 10 x 13-inch glass baking dish, add chicken stock, cream, garlic and parsley. Stir gently to mix. Add carrots and peas, stir gently to mix. Place chicken breasts on top of tomato mix. Bake for 35–40 minutes (or until chicken is done). Remove from oven, serve immediately.

Alternatively, remove chicken from dish, shred and mix back in with cream and vegetables to make a stew. Pour stew over warm biscuits and serve. (It's very similar to a pot pie!)

HONEY DIJON LIME CHICKEN

Yield: Serves 8

Ingredients:

2 whole chickens, pieced
½ cup Dijon mustard
¼ cup lime juice
2 Tbsp. honey

Preheat grill to medium heat. In a small bowl, mix mustard, lime juice and honey. Generously baste chicken with mustard sauce. Grill, turning chicken every 10 minutes until done. Baste regularly with mustard sauce while grilling. When finished cooking, remove and serve immediately with your favorite sides.

SLOW COOKER CHICKEN GOULASH
Yield: Serves 4–6

An Old World recipe, this is the perfect dish for using hens butchered after their egg-laying production has ended. My grandma Jo often baked this tender, flavorful dish. I've revised the process to a slow cooker version, which completely tenderizes any tough piece of chicken.

Ingredients:

4 lbs. chicken, boneless and skinless
2 cups Freezer Chicken Stock (page 95)
1 cup sour cream
2 onions, chopped
2 green bell peppers, seeded and chopped
2 tomatoes, diced
4 carrots, chopped
3 cloves of garlic, minced
¼ cup all-purpose flour
2 Tbsp. paprika, ground
1 Tbsp. caraway seeds
2 Tbsp. olive oil
Salt and pepper

In a 6-or 7-quart slow cooker (crock pot) add onions, tomatoes, green pepper, and carrots.

Chop chicken into 1-inch cubes. Heat olive oil in a large cast iron skillet over medium heat. Add chicken; sauté until all sides are browned. Remove from heat. Add chicken over the vegetable layer in the slow cooker.

Using the same large cast iron skillet the chicken was browned in, add stock. Stir over medium heat for 2 minutes. Add flour, paprika, caraway seeds, garlic, and a pinch of salt and pepper. Increase heat to high and bring mix to a boil, stirring continuously for 2 minutes. Remove from heat, and pour over chicken in slow cooker.

Cover slow cooker and cook on low setting for 8 hours. Stir in sour cream. Ladle hot goulash into bowls or serve over cooked rice or egg noodles.

7. Get Fed:

Preparing Your Garden Harvest

Organically grown vegetables and fruits fresh from the garden are simply the bee's knees! In a perfect gardening world, all produce picked could be consumed the same day, but our bounties are often much more plentiful than we plan for.

Most vegetables and fruits will remain fresh for several days and others up to several weeks with proper storage. To keep them longer, turn to Chapter 5: Get Cured for long-term storage techniques.

May be stored at room temperature (above 60 degrees) in shaded area

Apples	Limes	Potatoes
Bananas	Melons	Rutabagas
Grapefruit	Onions	Squash
Lemons	Oranges	Sweet potatoes

Refrigerated, uncovered, in or outside of produce bin

Apples	Cherries	Peaches
Apricots	Corn (in husks)	Pears
Avocados	Grapes	Peas (in pod)
Berries	Nectarines	Tomatoes

Refrigerated, covered, in or outside of produce bin

Asparagus	Carrots	Green beans
Beets	Cauliflower	Green onions
Bell peppers	Celery	Peas (shelled)
Broccoli	Corn (husked)	Radishes
Cabbage	Cucumber	Turnips

 Chick Tip: If necessary, shake off dirt and clean gently with a dry cloth when storing fresh vegetables. Do not wash prior to storing. Wash produce prior to using when removed from refrigerator. Washing before placing in refrigerator encourages mold development and spoilage.

AROUND THE GARDEN IN THIRTY DISHES

Most fresh veggies and fruits are naturally fabulous right off the vine, but when you have an abundant crop it's also rewarding to change things up with creative side dishes and vegetable main courses. Before you can all that fresh goodness, try these some of these fabulous recipes, many that will satisfy even the finickiest eaters (aka a terrific way to get your children to eat their vegetables!).

STUFFED ACORN SQUASH
Yield: Serves 4–6

Ingredients:

*4 acorn squash, seeded and cut
   in half*
2 cups cranberries
1 cup orange juice
½ cup white sugar
½ cup brown sugar
1 Tbsp. cinnamon

Preheat oven to 350 degrees Fahrenheit.

Warm a large cast iron skillet over medium heat. Add cranberries, orange juice, and white sugar. Cook for 10 minutes, stirring regularly. Remove from heat.

Line the bottom of a Dutch oven with acorn squash, skin side down. Dust squash with brown sugar, then cinnamon. Fill center of each squash with cranberry sauce. Cover Dutch oven and bake for 50 minutes or until squash is tender. Remove from oven, cool on baking rack for 10 minutes, then serve.

ASPARAGUS AU GRATIN
Yield: Serves 4–6

Ingredients:
2 lbs. fresh asparagus, chopped
½ cup green onions, minced
2 cups light cream
1 cup Parmesan cheese, grated
½ cup Swiss cheese, grated
4 Tbsp. butter
Salt

In a medium saucepan over medium heat, add water and a pinch of salt. Cook asparagus in water for 10 minutes (or until just tender). Drain asparagus, set aside.

Preheat oven to 375 degrees Fahrenheit.

In a large saucepan over medium heat, add butter, and heat until frothy. Add green onions; sauté until soft. Add cream. Stir continuously until cream is heated and slightly thickens. Add Parmesan and Swiss. Stir continuously until cheese is fully melted and incorporated. Remove from heat.

In a 10 x 13-inch baking dish, layer asparagus evenly across. Pour cheese sauce over asparagus. Bake for 25–30 minutes (or until cheese sauce is bubbled and lightly browned on top). Remove from oven. Allow to cool for 5 minutes, then serve.

BLACKBERRY BEET SOUP

Yield: Serves 4-6

Ingredients:

2 cups beets, peeled and chopped
1 potato, peeled and chopped
6 cups Freezer Chicken Stock
  (page 95)
2 cups applesauce
1 cup blackberries, mashed
2 sweet onions, diced
2 cloves of garlic, diced
1 Tbsp. sugar
1 Tbsp. cumin, ground
2 Tbsp. butter
½ cup port wine
Salt and pepper

Heat butter in a Dutch oven over medium heat until frothy. Add onions and garlic; sauté until soft. Add beets and potato, and cook for 10 minutes, stirring occasionally. Add chicken stock, applesauce, sugar, and cumin. Bring soup to a boil, then reduce heat to medium-low. Cover and cook for 15 minutes. Remove from heat.

Using a food processor, puree soup a few cups at a time. Transfer puree into a bowl to hold until all parts are pureed. Return pureed soup to Dutch oven. Add blackberries and port wine. Cook over medium-low heat, stirring regularly until heated. Remove from heat, ladle into soup bowls, and serve immediately.

SUNNY BROCCOLI SALAD

Yield: Serves 8-10

Ingredients:

4 cups broccoli tips, chopped
½ cup fried bacon, crumbled
½ cup sunflower seeds, shelled
½ cup golden raisins, chopped
1 red onion, diced
1 cup mayonnaise
4 Tbsp. vinegar
2 Tbsp. sugar

In a large bowl, add bacon, broccoli, sunflower seeds, raisins, and onion. Stir gently to mix.

In a small bowl, add mayonnaise, vinegar, and sugar. Whisk until dressing ingredients are fully incorporated. Pour over broccoli and toss until broccoli is fully coated with dressing. Chill in refrigerator for 1 hour prior to serving.

BAKED BRUSSELS SPROUTS

Yield: Serves 4

Ingredients:

2 cups Brussels sprouts
4 cups Freezer Chicken Stock
  (page 95)
½ cup Parmesan cheese
½ Tbsp. oregano, ground
½ Tbsp. basil, ground
½ Tbsp. salt

In a medium saucepan over medium-high heat, add chicken stock. When stock is hot, add Brussels sprouts. Reduce heat to medium and cook sprouts until tender. Remove from heat, drain sprouts, reserving ½ cup of chicken stock.

Preheat oven to 375 degrees Fahrenheit.

In a 10 x 13-inch glass pan, add sprouts and spread evenly across pan. Mix oregano and basil into ½ cup of reserved chicken stock. Pour stock over Brussels sprouts. Sprinkle Parmesan cheese evenly over Brussels sprouts. Bake 15 minutes or until cheese is browned. Remove and serve immediately.

ORCHARD CABBAGE

Yield: Serves 8

Ingredients:

1 head of cabbage, shredded

4 red apples, peeled, cored, and diced

1 pear, peeled, cored, and diced

1 onion, diced

1 cup brown sugar

1 cup vinegar

1 cup water

1 Tbsp. butter

Heat butter in a Dutch oven over medium heat until frothy. Add apples, pear, and onion; sauté until all are soft and lightly browned. Add cabbage and water. Cook 15 minutes or until cabbage is tender. Add brown sugar and vinegar, and stir gently until sugar is melted and ingredients are combined. Remove from heat. Cabbage may be served hot or allowed to cool and then served chilled. Either way is great!

STUFFED CARROT SOUP

Yield: Serves 4–6

Ingredients:

2 cups carrots, peeled and diced

2 cups potatoes, peeled and diced

4 cups Freezer Chicken Stock (page 95)

1 onion, diced

1 clove garlic, minced

½ tsp. pepper, ground

½ tsp. salt

2 Tbsp. butter

½ cup mild cheddar cheese, shredded

Heat butter in a large Dutch oven over medium heat until frothy. Add carrots, potatoes, garlic, and onions; sauté until carrots and onions are soft. Add chicken stock, salt, and pepper; simmer for 30 minutes, stirring regularly. (Reduce heat to medium-low if stock begins to boil.) Remove from heat, ladle into bowls, top each serving with a sprinkle of cheddar cheese, and serve immediately.

ROASTED CAULIFLOWER
Yield: Serves 6-8

Ingredients:
6 cups cauliflower florets
2 cloves of garlic, minced
1 Tbsp. lemon juice
3 Tbsp. olive oil
1 tsp. pepper, ground

Preheat oven to 400 degrees Fahrenheit.

In a large mixing bowl add garlic, lemon juice, oil, and pepper. Stir until fully combined. Add cauliflower; toss until cauliflower is fully coated with mix.

Transfer cauliflower to a 9 x 13-inch glass baking dish, spreading florets evenly across the dish. Bake for 15 minutes. Turn cauliflower over, and bake for 10–15 minutes or until florets are lightly browned. Remove from oven, and serve immediately.

FRESH CORN FRITTER PATTIES
Yield: Serves 4–6

Ingredients:
*2 cups fresh corn, removed from
    cob*
2 Tbsp. light cream
2 eggs
¼ cup all-purpose flour
Salt and pepper
Canola oil

Fill a medium cast iron frying pan one quarter way full with canola oil. Heat oil over medium heat.

Separate egg yolks from whites. In a large mixing bowl, mix egg yolks with corn, cream, and a pinch of salt and pepper. Stir until eggs are fully combined. Add flour; stir until batter is formed.

In a small mixing bowl, beat egg whites until they form stiff peaks. Add egg whites to corn mixture, gently mixing into batter.

Drop heaping tablespoons of batter into heated oil. (Be sure to drop batter in close to oil to avoid splashing.) Fry corn fritter, flipping once to brown both sides. Remove fritter from oil with a slotted spoon, allowing any excess oil to drip back into frying pan. Serve while still warm.

CUCUMBER AND GREEN BEAN SALAD

Yield: Serves 4

Ingredients:

4 cups green beans, trimmed and halved

1 cucumber, peeled and chopped

1 green onion, chopped fine

2 Tbsp. fresh rosemary, chopped

2 Tbsp. fresh parsley, chopped fine

1 tsp. lemon juice

½ tsp. English mustard

¼ cup olive oil

½ cup feta cheese

½ cups water

Salt and pepper

In a medium saucepan, over high heat, add water and rosemary and bring to a boil. Reduce heat to medium-high. Cool green beans for 5 minutes. Remove from heat and drain.

In a small mixing bowl, add onion, parsley, lemon juice, mustard, olive oil, and a pinch of salt and pepper. Whisk until dressing ingredients are fully incorporated.

In a large bowl, add green beans and cucumber. Pour dressing over beans and cucumbers; toss until vegetables are coated with dressing. Add feta cheese, and gently toss. Serve portions in salad bowls.

EGGPLANT DIP

Yield: Serves 10–12

Ingredients:

*2 large eggplants, washed and
    sliced in half lengthwise*
2 Tbsp. parsley, chopped fine
2 cloves of garlic, minced
1 Tbsp. lemon juice
4 Tbsp. olive oil, plus 1 tsp.
1 tsp. sea salt

Preheat oven to broil.

Rub flesh side of eggplant halves with ¼ tsp. olive oil. Place eggplant, flesh side down, on a baking sheet. Roast in oven for 30 minutes, or until eggplant skin is blackened and eggplant is soft. Remove from oven; cool on baking rack for 10 minutes. Remove skin from eggplant and discard (compost). Place flesh of eggplant in a medium mixing bowl and mash. Set aside to cool for ½ hour.

In a food processor, add mashed eggplant, parsley, garlic lemon juice, 4 Tbsp. olive oil, and sea salt. Process until smooth. Transfer to a dip bowl. Serve with crudités, crackers, or flat bread.

GREENS AND BEANS

Yield: Serves 6–8

Ingredients:

*8 cups white beans (cannelloni
    or great northern, presoaked,
    rinsed, and drained)*
*4 cups fresh greens (collard or
    turnip, washed and chopped)*
*4 cups Freezer Chicken Stock
    (page 95)*
1 onion, diced
1 Tbsp. olive oil

Heat oil in a large Dutch oven over medium heat. Add onions and sauté until soft. Add beans, greens, and chicken stock. Cook for 45 minutes, stirring occasionally. If liquid begins to boil, reduce heat to medium-low. Remove from heat; strain beans and greens from stock and serve immediately. (Alternatively, beans and greens may be served in stock as a soup.)

EASY GARDEN GAZPACHO
Yield: Serves 4

Ingredients:

1 cup tomato puree

4 Roma tomatoes, peeled and
chopped

1 clove garlic

1 cucumber, peeled and chopped

1 red pepper, seeded and
chopped

4 Tbsp. olive oil

4 Tbsp. red wine vinegar

1 cup Brown Bread (page 200),
cubed

Salt and pepper

Water

Using a food processor, add tomatoes, tomato puree, garlic, cucumber, red pepper, olive oil, and red wine vinegar. Pulse until coarsely chopped. Add ½ cup of water; process until smooth. Add brown bread and ¼ cup water, process until smooth.

Pour gazpacho into a storage container. Chill in refrigerator for 2 hours. Ladle into bowls, serve, and enjoy.

GREEK STYLE GREEN BEANS

Yield: Serves 4

Ingredients:
*2 cups fresh green beans,
    trimmed*
1 cup cherry or grape tomatoes
6 cloves garlic, minced
1 small onion, diced
¼ tsp. cayenne, ground
1 tsp. fresh rosemary, chopped
4 Tbsp. olive oil
½ cup feta cheese, crumbled
4 cups water

In a large saucepan over high heat, add water and bring to a boil. Add green beans; cook for 5–6 minutes (until just tender). Remove from heat, drain, and set aside.

Heat oil in a large cast iron skillet over medium heat. Add onions and garlic; sauté until soft. Add cayenne, rosemary, and tomatoes; sauté for 2 minutes. Add green beans, stirring gently for 2 minutes. Remove from heat, transfer to serving tray. Sprinkle with feta cheese, and serve immediately.

CREAM OF MUSHROOM SOUP

Yield: Serves 4-6

Ingredients:
*2 cups white button mushrooms,
    washed, dried, and chopped*
*3 cups Freezer Chicken Stock
    (page 95)*
1 cup heavy cream
3 Tbsp. butter
2 Tbsp. all-purpose flour
1 Tbsp. fresh thyme, minced
1 Tbsp. fresh parsley, minced
½ Tbsp. pepper, ground

Heat butter in a large Dutch oven over medium heat until frothy. Add flour, and stir frequently until a paste is formed. Add ½ cup chicken stock, stirring regularly until paste is incorporated and stock is thickened. Increase heat to high, add remainder of chicken stock, and bring to a boil. Reduce heat to medium-low, add mushrooms, and simmer for 10 minutes. Add cream, thyme, parsley, and pepper. Simmer for 5 minutes, stirring regularly. Remove from heat, ladle into bowls, and serve immediately.

OLD COUNTRY FRENCH ONION SOUP

Yield: Serves 4-6

Ingredients:
6 red onions, sliced thin
6 cups beef broth
3 Tbsp. flour
4 Tbsp. butter
2 Tbsp. cornstarch
Salt and pepper
Parmesan cheese, grated
Brown Bread (page 200), sliced,
*   toasted and cubed*

Heat butter in a Dutch oven over medium heat until frothy. Add onions; sauté until soft and fully browned. Add flour, and simmer for 2 minutes, stirring regularly. Add beef broth and a pinch of salt and pepper; cook for 30 minutes.

While soup is cooking, in a small bowl, add cornstarch and ½ cup of water. Mix until cornstarch is fully dissolved.

When soup is done cooking, add cornstarch. Stir gently until thickened. Remove from heat. Ladle into soup bowls, top with shredded cheese and brown bread cubes, and serve immediately.

BARBECUE LIMA BEANS
Yield: Serves 4–6

I know very few people, including myself, who will race to request lima beans for supper. This dish will change that reluctance lickety-split. Serve at your next barbecue, and watch how quickly everyone reaches for a second helping!

Ingredients:

1 cup lima beans
¼ cup onion, peeled and
  chopped
2 cloves of garlic, chopped
1 slice thick cut bacon, chopped
½ cup tomatoes, peeled and
  pureed
1 Tbsp. yellow mustard
1 Tbsp. vinegar
1 tsp. brown sugar
½ tsp. Worcestershire sauce
½ tsp. chili powder
2 cups water

In a medium saucepan, over high heat, add water and lima beans; bring to a boil. Boil for 2 minutes. Remove from heat and set aside for 1 hour. Return saucepan to stove. Over medium-high heat, bring to a boil, reduce heat to medium, and boil gently until lima beans are fully tender. Remove from heat and drain beans, reserving ½ cup of water.

Preheat oven to 400 degrees Fahrenheit.

In a medium cast iron skillet, over medium heat, add bacon, onion, and garlic. Sauté until bacon, onion, and garlic are tender and lightly browned. Add lima beans, water from beans, and all remaining ingredients. Stir until fully combined. Transfer skillet from stovetop to oven. Bake for 30 minutes. Remove from oven, cool for 10 minutes, then serve.

MINTED PEAS

Yield: Serves 4-6

Ingredients:
4 cups peas, shelled
¼ cup mint leaves, chopped
2 Tbsp. butter
Water
Salt

In a medium saucepan over medium heat, add peas. Cover peas with water and add a pinch of salt. Increase heat to high, and boil peas until tender. Remove from heat.

In a medium bowl add butter, mint, and a pinch of salt. Drain peas and add hot peas to bowl. Stir gently until butter is fully melted and peas are coated. Serve immediately.

SASSY SUGAR SNAP PEAS

Yield: Serves 4-6

Ingredients:
2 cups sugar snap peas in pod,
*   trimmed*
2 shallots, chopped
1 orange bell pepper, seeded and
*   chopped*
3 cloves of garlic, minced
¼ cup Orange Tangerine
*   Marmalade (page 114)*
2 Tbsp. olive oil
Salt and pepper

Heat oil in a large cast iron skillet over medium heat. Add garlic; sauté 2 minutes. Add onion, pepper and a pinch of salt and pepper, and sauté until all vegetables are tender. Add pea pods, and sauté until pods are tender. Remove from heat. Add marmalade, stir until fully incorporated, and serve immediately.

OLIVE POTATO SALAD
Yield: Serves 8

Ingredients:

4 lbs. red potatoes, peeled and
　　cubed
½ cup green olives, sliced
¼ cup red onion, diced
¾ cup mayonnaise
¼ cup sour cream
2 Tbsp. whole grain mustard
1 tsp. fresh dill, chopped thin
Salt and pepper
Water

In a large Dutch oven, over medium heat, add potatoes and a pinch of salt. Cover potatoes with water. Increase heat to high and boil potatoes until tender (but not fork soft). Remove from heat. Drain potatoes and cool for 1 hour.

In a large mixing bowl, add potatoes, mayonnaise, sour cream, onion, olives, dill, and a pinch of salt and pepper. Gently stir until fully mixed. Chill potato salad in refrigerator for 4 hours, scoop, and serve.

HERB GARDEN RADISHES
Yield: Serves 4

Ingredients:

2 cups radishes, sliced
1 Tbsp. fresh mint, chopped
1 Tbsp. fresh parsley, chopped
1 Tbsp. chives, chopped
1 Tbsp. basil, chopped
4 Tbsp. olive oil
1 Tbsp. lemon juice

Heat oil in a large cast iron skillet over medium heat. Add radishes, mint, parsley, chives, and basil. Sauté until radishes are tender and lightly browned. Add lemon juice; cook for 1 minute, stirring gently. Remove from heat, and serve immediately.

SPICED RED CABBAGE

Yield: Serves 8–10

Ingredients:
1 head red cabbage, shredded
4 scallions, sliced
1 green chili, seeded and sliced
   thin
¼ cup fresh cilantro, chopped
¼ cup lemon juice
¼ cup olive oil
2 Tbsp. red wine vinegar
1 Tbsp. sea salt

In a small bowl, add lemon juice, chili, oil, and vinegar. Whisk until dressing ingredients are combined.

In a large bowl, add cabbage, scallions, cilantro, salt, and dressing. Toss until cabbage is fully coated with dressing. Serve immediately.

SAVORY SUMMER SQUASH

Yield: Serves 4

Ingredients:
2 yellow summer squash, sliced
   thin
2 cloves garlic, minced
3 Tbsp. low-sodium soy sauce
1 tsp. ginger, ground
2 Tbsp. olive oil

Heat oil in a large cast iron skillet over medium heat. Add garlic; sauté until soft and lightly browned. Add summer squash and ginger; sauté until soft. Reduce heat to low, add soy sauce, and gently stir. Cover and simmer for 5 minutes. Remove from heat, and serve immediately.

HERBED SWEET POTATOES

Yield: Serves 4

Ingredients:

4 sweet potatoes
¼ cup light cream
2 Tbsp. butter
1 Tbsp. brown sugar
1 tsp. cinnamon, ground
1 tsp. thyme, ground
¼ cup black walnuts, shelled and
  chopped
Water

In a large Dutch oven, over medium heat, add sweet potatoes. Cover potatoes with water. Increase heat to high and boil potatoes until soft. Remove from heat. Drain sweet potatoes and peel.

In a medium mixing bowl, add sweet potatoes, cream, butter, brown sugar, thyme, and cinnamon. Mash until ingredients are fully mixed. (If mash is too thick, add a little extra light cream to thin.) Scoop onto plates, sprinkle black walnuts over sweet potatoes, and serve.

MEDITERRANEAN STUFFED TOMATOES

Yield: Serves 4

Ingredients:

4 large tomatoes
1 onion, chopped
2 scallions, chopped
1 clove garlic, minced
1 Tbsp. raisins, chopped
1 Tbsp. fresh oregano, chopped
1 Tbsp. fresh dill, chopped
1 Tbsp. fresh mint, chopped
2 Tbsp. olive oil
1 cup cooked red quinoa
¼ cups water
Salt and pepper

Preheat oven to 400 degrees Fahrenheit.

Cut tops from tomatoes. Set aside. Using a spoon, carefully scoop seeds and loose pulp from tomatoes into a food processor, leaving a solid shell. Set tomato shell aside. Puree seeds and pulp in food processor. Set aside.

Heat oil in a large cast iron skillet oven over medium heat. Add onion, and sauté until soft. Add garlic, scallions, oregano, dill, raisins, and mint, and sauté for 2 minutes. Add red quinoa; sauté for 2 minutes. Remove from heat. Add tomato puree and a pinch of salt and pepper. Stir gently until stuffing is combined.

In an 8 x 8-inch baking dish, place tomato shells, with the open side facing upward. Scoop equal amounts of stuffing into the cavity of each tomato shell. Place tops of tomatoes atop the stuffing (as if you were putting the tomato back together). Pour water around the tomatoes in bottom of baking dish. Bake for 40 minutes. Remove from oven, cool on baking rack for 10–15 minutes, then serve.

TOMATILLO PIE
Yield: Serves 4–6

The first time I grew tomatillos, I had no idea what an abundance of fruit one plant would produce. There's only so much salsa and sauce I could store or gift, so I had to find alternative ways to enjoy them. Swapping tomatillos into one of my favorite tomato pie recipes turned out to be a fabulous decision. Serve as a light summer lunch or as a side to your favorite Mexican-style dishes.

Ingredients:

4 ripe tomatillos, diced
4 eggs
1 clove garlic, diced
1 shallot, diced
2 Tbsp. butter
4 Tbsp. Italian-style seasoned bread crumbs
1 Tbsp. olive oil
½ cup sharp cheddar cheese, shredded
¼ cup Monterey cheese, shredded

Heat oven to 350 degrees Fahrenheit.

Use butter to grease the sides and bottom of a 9-inch pie pan. Sprinkle the bread crumbs over the bottom of the pan and lightly shake to cover the sides and bottom. Tap out the remaining bread crumbs and reserve for later.

Heat oil in a large cast iron skillet over medium heat. Add onions and garlic; sauté until soft. Add diced tomatillos and simmer for 5 minutes, stirring frequently. Remove from heat; set aside.

In medium mixing bowl, add eggs and cheese. Whisk until eggs are frothy.

Spoon tomatillo mixture into pie pan, spreading it evenly across bottom. Pour egg mixture on top of tomatillo layer, and spread evenly. Sprinkle remaining bread crumbs on top of egg layer. Bake for 30 minutes (crumbs should be browned on top). Remove and cool on cooling rack for 10 minutes. Slice into wedges and serve.

LATE-SUMMER VEGETABLE SOUP

Yield: Serves 8–10

Ingredients:

2 cups carrots, peeled and
*   chopped*
1 cup celery, chopped
2 cups potatoes, peeled and
*   chopped*
2 cups green beans, trimmed and
*   chopped*
2 cups corn
1 cup okra, seeded and chopped
4 cups tomatoes, chopped
1 cup sweet onions, chopped
1 Tbsp. fresh parsley, chopped
1 Tbsp. fresh thyme, chopped
2 Tbsp. apple cider vinegar
2 Tbsp. olive oil
2 cups water

Heat oil in a Dutch oven over medium heat. Add onion and garlic; sauté until tender and browned. Add all vegetables, herbs, and vinegar. Stir gently. Increase heat to medium-high and bring to a boil. Cover Dutch oven and reduce heat to low. Cook 20 minutes. Add water; stir gently to incorporate. Cover and cook for 25 minutes. Remove from heat, uncover and cool on trivet for 10 minutes. Ladle into soup bowls and serve.

AUTUMN VEGETABLE SALAD

Yield: Serves 4–6

Ingredients:

*2 sweet potatoes, peeled and
　chopped*
*2 tart apples, peeled, cored and
　chopped*
½ cup raisins
*1 cup pecans, shelled and
　chopped*
2 tsp. ginger root, minced
1 tsp. cinnamon, ground
½ tsp. nutmeg, ground
¼ cup olive oil plus 2 Tbsp.
2 Tbsp. apple cider vinegar
2 Tbsp. orange juice
2 Tbsp. pure maple syrup
1 Tbsp. lemon juice
Salt and pepper

Preheat oven to 400 degrees Fahrenheit.

In a large mixing bowl, add sweet potatoes, 2 Tbsp. olive oil, and a pinch of salt and pepper. Toss gently to coat sweet potatoes. Layer sweet potatoes evenly across the bottom of a 10 x 13-inch glass baking pan. Bake for 30 minutes. Remove from oven. Cool on baking rack for 30 minutes.

In a large mixing bowl, add olive oil, vinegar, orange juice, maple syrup, lemon juice, and ginger root. Whisk until fully combined. Add sweet potatoes, apples, raisins, and pecans. Toss lightly to mix and serve.

MINTED GRILLED ZUCCHINI

Yield: Serves 4

Ingredients:

2 large zucchini

2 Tbsp. mint leaves, diced

2 Tbsp. olive oil

2 Tbsp. lemon juice

Sea salt

Cut zucchini across the middle to form two circular halves. Cut each half into 1-inch wide spears.

In a small bowl, add mint leaves, olive oil, sea salt, and lemon juice. Using a large, zippered bag or marinating tray, add zucchini and marinade. Gently shake zucchini with marinade until zucchini is fully coated. Allow zucchini to rest in marinade for 15 minutes.

Preheat grill to medium heat. Grill zucchini spears, turning frequently until thoroughly heated and softened. Remove from heat and serve immediately.

 Chick Tip: Harvest zucchini blossoms in the morning, when they have just opened. Do not use flowers that have pesticides or marks of deterioration. Large blossoms with ½-inch to 1-inch stems (trim any excess) will prepare well and offer the ideal taste.

FRIED ZUCCHINI FLOWERS

Yield: Serves 4

Ingredients:

2 cups zucchini blossoms,
*   cleaned and dried*
2 eggs, beaten
1 cup all-purpose flour
¼ cup bread crumbs
1 tsp. oregano, ground
1 cup canola oil
½ tsp. salt
½ tsp. pepper, ground

Heat oil in a large cast iron skillet over medium heat.

In a small mixing bowl, combine bread crumbs, flour, oregano, salt, and pepper. Dredge zucchini blossoms through eggs, allowing excess to drip off. Dredge blossoms through flour mix, covering completely. Drop floured blossoms into oil. Cook, turning often, until lightly browned on all sides. Remove from oil, allow excess oil to drain off, and serve immediately.

8. Get Baked:

Creating Artisan Breads and Sweets

Whether you are complementing a meal, soup, or simply a cup of tea, fresh breads and baked goods are a heavenly addition to the menu. Most of my bread making is highly influenced by my Irish roots. Some skills, like the art of scone making, I brought back home with me from my travels in Ireland.

Personally, I think Irish artisan breads and sweets are highly underappreciated due to their simplicity, but it is this less complicated process that showcases each ingredient. The elegance and emphasis of bringing out each natural flavor is what makes them so delightful.

BROWN BREAD
Yield: 1 loaf

Ingredients:

*2 cups whole wheat four (or Irish-
style whole meal flour)*
¼ cup all-purpose flour
¼ cup uncooked oats, plus 2 Tbsp.
3 eggs
2 cups buttermilk (or whole milk)
2 tsp. baking soda
2 tsp. canola oil
Salt

Preheat oven to 350 degrees Fahrenheit.

In a large mixing bowl, add whole wheat flour and all-purpose flour; mix gently. Add baking soda, ¼ cup oats and a pinch of salt; mix gently to incorporate.

In a medium mixing bowl, add eggs, and beat until frothy. Add oil; whisk until combined. Add buttermilk; whisk until combined. Pour egg mixture into flour mix, and stir until fully combined. Dough will be runny.

Grease a standard 2-pound bread loaf pan. Pour dough into bread pan, bake for ½ hour. Sprinkle 2 Tbsp. of oats evenly across the top of the loaf. Bake for 45 minutes. Remove from oven. Allow to cool for 5 minutes. Remove from loaf pan and cool on a wire rack for 10 minutes, then slice and serve.

If you prefer bread at room temperature rather than hot, allow bread to cool for 1 hour prior to slicing. Once cooled, bread may be rewarmed in a toaster, toaster oven, or microwave (5–10 minute setting).

If it lasts past the first day, brown bread may be stored in an airtight container in a cool location for up to 5 days.

Chick Tip: Unless a recipe specifically requests it, do not sift your flour. Spoon flour into a glass measuring cup to help avoid air pockets and lumps. If necessary, level the flour gently with a straight edge to obtain an accurate measurement.

BROWN BREAD CRUMBS

Yield: Will vary by amount of bread and thickness of slices.

Preheat oven to 250 degrees Fahrenheit.

Slice day-old bread (or 2–3 day-old bread) into ½-inch slices. Lay slices onto cookie sheets. Dry in oven, turning slices every 15 minutes until bread is crisp. Remove bread from oven and cool for 30 minutes.

Transfer bread to a clean, dry, flat surface. Using a rolling pin, flatten bread until crumbed. Transfer bread crumbs to an airtight container. Store in a cool, dry, dark location for up to one week.

Optional: use an airtight freezer container or airtight freezer bag to store breadcrumbs in the freezer for up to one year.

GRANDMA JO'S ORANGE CARROT BREAD
Yield: 1 loaf

When I was young, my grandparents moved to Florida to retire, which fortunately for me meant I got to spend many a summer hanging out in the Sunshine State. Ever the resourceful one, Grandma Jo found ways to add plenty of fresh citrus, the abundant local crop, into her recipes. My grandmother says this recipe is also "great for the bones" and an easy way to get children to eat veggies. I think she was certainly onto something!

Ingredients:
1 cup whole wheat flour
1 cup all-purpose flour
1¼ cup carrots, grated
½ cup fresh orange juice
⅓ cup applesauce
¼ cup sugar
1 egg
1 tsp. pure vanilla extract
2 tsp. cinnamon, ground
½ tsp. cloves, ground
¼ tsp. nutmeg, ground
1 tsp. baking powder
½ tsp. baking soda
¼ tsp. salt

Preheat oven to 350 degrees Fahrenheit.

In a large mixing bowl, add orange juice, applesauce, sugar, egg, and vanilla. Whisk ingredients until fully combined. Set aside.

In a medium mixing bowl, add wheat flour, flour, cinnamon, cloves, nutmeg, baking powder, baking soda, and salt. Stir until ingredients are fully incorporated.

Slowly add dry ingredients to wet ingredients, stirring gently until fully combined. Add carrots, and gently fold into batter until fully incorporated.

Pour batter into a greased 9 x 5-inch loaf pan. Bake for 45 minutes or until bread is fully set. Remove from oven; cool on baking rack for 10 minutes. Remove bread from pan; cool on baking rack for 45 minutes. Serve slightly warm or cool. Refrigerate leftovers in an airtight container for up to 1 week.

APPLESAUCE BREAD

Yield: 1 loaf

Ingredients:

2 cups all-purpose flour
1½ cups applesauce
1 cup sugar
¼ cup brown sugar
2 eggs
3 Tbsp. milk
¾ cup pecans, chopped
1 tsp. baking soda
½ tsp. baking powder
1 tsp. cinnamon, ground
½ tsp. nutmeg, ground

Preheat oven to 350 degrees Fahrenheit.

In a large mixing bowl, add flour, baking soda, baking powder, cinnamon, and nutmeg, and mix gently.

In a medium-sized mixing bowl, add applesauce, sugar, eggs, and milk; blend thoroughly. Add applesauce mix to flour, and stir gently until fully blended. Add ½ cup of pecans; fold in gently to incorporate.

Pour bread mix into a greased 9 x 5-inch loaf pan.

In a small bowl, mix ¼ cup pecans and brown sugar. Sprinkle evenly over bread.

Bake for 1 hour. Remove from oven; cool for 5 minutes. Remove bread from loaf pan and cool on baker's rack for 30 minutes. Slice and serve.

CLASSIC GINGERBREAD
Yield: 1 loaf

Ingredients:

2½ cups all-purpose flour
1 cup molasses
½ cup sugar
½ cup butter, softened
1 tsp. baking soda
1 tsp. cinnamon, ground
½ tsp. cloves, ground
½ tsp. ginger, ground
1 cup hot water

Preheat oven to 325 degrees Fahrenheit.

In a large mixing bowl, add butter and sugar. Beat until fully mixed and smooth. Add egg and molasses. Beat until fully mixed and smooth. Add flour, baking soda, cinnamon, cloves, and ginger. Stir gently until flour is fully incorporated. Mixture will be stiff. Add hot water, and beat until fully mixed and batter-like.

Pour bread mix into a greased 9 x 5-inch loaf pan. Bake for 30 minutes or until center of bread is fully set. Remove from oven; cool for 5 minutes. Remove from loaf pan and cool on baker's rack for 30 minutes. Slice and serve.

WINE BISCUITS
Yield: 2 dozen

Ingredients:
4 cups whole wheat flour
1 cup sugar
1 cup butter
½ cup red table wine
4 tsp. baking powder
1 tsp. baking soda

Preheat oven to 350 degrees Fahrenheit.

In a large mixing bowl, add flour, baking soda, and baking powder; stir gently until combined.

In a medium mixing bowl, add sugar and butter; cream until smooth and fully combined. Add wine, and cream until wine is incorporated. Add half of flour mix; stir until fully mixed. Add remainder of the flour; stir until fully mixed.

Drop dough by tablespoons onto a greased or nonstick cookie sheet, leaving a 1-inch space between dough drops. Bake for 10 minutes or until edges of wine biscuits are lightly browned. Remove from oven, remove from tray, and cool on baking rack for 5 minutes prior to serving. Wine biscuits may also be cooled completely and served at room temperature.

ROLLED OAT CAKES WITH BLACKBERRY BOURBON SAUCE

Yield: 3–4 dozen

Ingredients:

1½ cups rolled oats
1½ cups all-purpose flour
½ cup sugar
½ tsp. baking soda
½ cup shortening
¼ cup water

Preheat oven to 350 degrees Fahrenheit.

In a large mixing bowl, add oats, flour, sugar, and baking soda. Stir until fully mixed. Using a pastry cutter, cut shortening into oat mix until fully crumbed. Add water and mix. You may add a little extra water if needed to fully wet ingredients, but do not add too much; dough should be stiff.

On a clean, flat, dry work surface, roll dough approximately half an inch thick. Sprinkle a few rolled oats on top of the dough and press in gently with a rolling pin. Using a cookie cutter or pastry knife, cut dough into 1-inch squares or circular shapes. Dough scraps may be rerolled to create additional cakes.

Transfer dough cut-outs to cookie sheets, leaving a 1-inch space between cut-outs. Bake for 15 minutes or until center is firm and edges are lightly browned. Remove from oven, and transfer cakes to baking rack to cool. Serve warm or cool with Blackberry Bourbon Sauce (page 207).

BLACKBERRY BOURBON SAUCE

Yield: 2 cups

Ingredients:

2 cups blackberries
½ cup bourbon
¼ cup sugar

In a medium saucepan over medium heat, add all ingredients. Cook for 15 minutes until fully heated, stirring regularly. Remove from heat; cool for 5 minutes.

Puree in a food processor until smooth. If sauce thickens too much, add a little warm water and pulse to thin. Serve warm or cooled. Sauce may be stored in the refrigerator for up to 2 weeks.

 Chick Tip: To achieve the fluffiest muffins and cakes, use only ingredients that are room temperature. An hour prior to baking, set out your butter, eggs, milk, or other refrigerated ingredients to allow them to reach room temperature before use.

BASIC MUFFIN RECIPE

Yield: 1 dozen

Ingredients:

2 cups all-purpose flour
½ cup milk
¼ cup butter, melted
½ cup sugar
1 egg
1 Tbsp. baking powder

Preheat oven to 400 degrees Fahrenheit.

In a large mixing bowl, add milk, butter, sugar, and egg. Beat until frothy. Add flour and baking powder, and stir until fully incorporated. Add flavor boosters from muffin chart below, as desired; stir to incorporate.

Pour muffin batter into greased muffin tins, filling muffin compartment half full. Bake for 20 minutes (or until tops are lightly browned). Remove from oven. Remove muffins from pan and cool on a baking rack. Serve warm or cool.

Use one of these flavor booster combinations to create fun muffin flavors, or experiment with ingredients to come up with your personal favorite muffin sensation.

To make...	Add these extras to the basic mix...		
Apple Cinnamon	½ cup apples, diced	½ cup walnuts, chopped	1 Tbsp. cinnamon, ground
Banana Nut	2 bananas, mashed	½ cup walnuts, chopped	1 tsp. nutmeg, ground
Blackberry Bourbon	1 cup blackberries	¼ cup bourbon	1 tsp. pure vanilla extract
Carrot Cake	½ cup carrots, grated	2 tsp. cinnamon, ground 1 tsp. nutmeg, ground	½ cup walnuts, chopped ¼ cup raisins
Cheddar Herb	½ cup sharp cheddar cheese, grated	¼ cup fresh parsley, chopped	2 Tbsp. fresh rosemary, chopped
Chocolate Strawberry	½ cup strawberries, diced	2 Tbsp. cocoa powder	½ cup semisweet chocolate chips
Citrus Dream	2 Tbsp. orange zest	3 Tbsp. lime juice	2 Tbsp. lemon zest
Cranberry Orange Nut	½ cup cranberries	2 Tbsp. orange zest	½ cup walnuts, chopped
Dark Chocolate Orange	¼ cup orange zest	1 tsp. pure vanilla extract	½ cup dark chocolate chips
Double Chocolate	¼ cup cocoa powder	1 tsp. pure vanilla extract	½ cup semisweet chocolate chip

Ginger Pear	½ cup pear, diced	1 Tbsp. ginger, ground	1 tsp. pure vanilla extract
Irish Coffee	½ cup cocoa powder	1 Tbsp. instant coffee granules	2 Tbsp. Irish cream liqueur
Mojito Magic	1 Tbsp. fresh mint, chopped thin	¼ cup lime zest 2 Tbsp. lime juice	½ cup white chocolate chips
PBJ Muffins	½ cup strawberry jam	½ cup peanut butter chips	1 tsp. pure vanilla extract
Peanut Butter Cup	½ cup semisweet chocolate chips	½ cup peanut butter chips	½ cup peanuts, chopped
Pumpkin Apple	1 cup pumpkin puree	½ cup apples, chopped	1 tsp. cinnamon, ground
Spiced Blueberry	½ cup blueberries	1 tsp. cinnamon, ground	1 tsp. nutmeg, ground
Strawberry Daiquiri	½ cup strawberries, diced	2 Tbsp. lime juice	2 Tbsp. strawberry rum
Sweet Potato Pecan	½ cup sweet potato, cooked and mashed	1 tsp. cinnamon, ground	½ cup pecans, chopped
White Raspberry	1 cup raspberries	1 tsp. pure vanilla extract	½ cup white chocolate chips
Zesty Spinach	½ cup fresh spinach, chopped	½ cup feta cheese, crumbled	1 Tbsp. fresh dill, chopped
Zucchini Nut	½ cup zucchini, grated	½ cup almonds, chopped	½ tsp. nutmeg, ground

BASIC IRISH SCONE RECIPE
Yield: 1–2 dozen

The primary difference between Southern-style biscuits and Irish scones is the egg in the mix.

Ingredients:
2 cups all-purpose flour
1 cup milk
2 eggs
½ cup butter

Preheat oven to 425 degrees Fahrenheit.

In a large mixing bowl, add flour and butter. Using a pastry cutter, cut butter into flour until fully crumbed. In a small mixing bowl, whisk eggs and milk until thoroughly combined. Pour mix into flour mix and stir until a soft dough is formed.

Transfer dough to a floured pastry sheet. Use a lightly floured rolling pin to gently flatten dough to 1-inch thickness. Using a round cookie cutter, cut scones from dough.

Place cut scones in a large cast iron skillet or cast iron pizza pan.

Gather remaining dough in a ball, reflatten with a rolling pin, then cut scones from dough. Repeat until entire batch of dough is cut into scones. If you have a little excess dough left, just pat it onto the top of the cut scones.

Bake for 12–15 minutes. Cool on wire rack. Serve warm or cooled with butter, jelly, jam, Dried Fruit Compote (page 218), or fresh cream.

SWEET SCONE RECIPE
Yield: 1–2 dozen

Ingredients:

2 cups all-purpose flour
1 cup milk
2 eggs
½ cup butter
¼ cup raisins (or chopped dates)
¼ cup dried cranberries
½ cup sugar
1 tsp. pure vanilla extract

Preheat oven to 425 degrees Fahrenheit.

In a large mixing bowl, add flour, sugar and butter. Using a pastry cutter, cut butter into flour and sugar until fully crumbed.

In a small mixing bowl, whisk eggs, vanilla and milk until thoroughly combined. Pour mix into flour mix and stir until a soft dough is formed. Add raisins and cranberries; stir gently until incorporated into the dough.

Proceed with Basic Irish Scone Recipe directions (page 211).

SAVORY SCONE RECIPE
Yield: 2 dozen

Ingredients:

2 cups all-purpose flour
1 cup milk
2 eggs
½ cup butter
½ cup sharp cheddar cheese
½ cup bacon, cooked and
   crumbled
1 tsp. garlic powder
1 tsp. rosemary, ground

Preheat oven to 425 degrees Fahrenheit.

In a large mixing bowl, add flour and butter. Using a pastry cutter, cut butter into flour and sugar until fully crumbed.

In a small mixing bowl, whisk eggs, milk, garlic and rosemary until thoroughly combined. Pour mix into flour mix and stir until a soft dough is formed. Add cheese and bacon; stir gently until incorporated into the dough.

Proceed with Basic Irish Scone Recipe directions (page 211).

POOR MAN'S SKILLET BRANDY CAKE
Yield: 1-2 dozen

Ingredients:
2 cups all-purpose flour
5 egg yolks
¼ cup heavy cream
3 Tbsp. brandy
3 Tbsp. confectioner's sugar
½ tsp. lemon peel, grated
½ tsp. ginger, ground
½ tsp. cinnamon, ground
4 cups canola oil (or preferred frying oil)

In a large mixing bowl, add eggs, and whisk until frothy. Add cream, sugar, brandy, lemon peel, ginger, and cinnamon; whisk until fully combined. Add flour, and stir until fully combined and dough is formed. Cover and chill mixture in refrigerator for 8 hours.

On a clean, flat, dry work surface, roll dough to approximately ⅛-inch thickness. Using a cookie cutter or pastry knife, cut dough into 2-inch circular shapes. Dough scraps may be rerolled to create additional cakes.

Heat oil in a large skillet over medium-high heat until a frying temperature of 370 degrees Fahrenheit is reached. Gently place dough rounds into oil, fry for 2 minutes or until dough is lightly browned on all sides. Remove from oil, set aside and continue frying until all cakes are done.

Sprinkle cakes with confectioner's sugar and serve warm or cooled.

MY MOM'S APPLE WALNUT BUNDT CAKE
Yield: 1 cake

The moist texture and rich combination of flavors made this cake one of my mom and dad's favorites to bake. When visiting, you could always count on a slice! My mother's secret to always having a made-from-scratch cake on hand is that this is an excellent freezer cake. When kept in an airtight wrapper or container, Apple Walnut Bundt Cake tastes just as fresh as the day it was baked when you take it out to defrost.

Ingredients:

3 cups all-purpose flour

3 eggs

3 medium Golden Delicious apples, peeled, cored, and chopped fine

1 cup walnuts, chopped

1 cup golden raisins

1 cup sugar

1 cup olive oil

½ cup apple juice

2 tsp. pure vanilla extract

1 tsp. baking soda

1 tsp. cinnamon, ground

¾ tsp. salt

¼ tsp. nutmeg, ground

Preheat oven to 350 degrees Fahrenheit. Grease and flour a 10-inch Bundt pan.

In a large mixing bowl, add flour, sugar, baking soda, cinnamon, salt, nutmeg, oil, apple juice, vanilla, and eggs. Beat ingredients until well blended and smooth. Add apples, walnuts, and raisins; gently fold into batter until fully incorporated.

Spoon batter into Bundt pan, distributing it evenly. Bake for 60 minutes or until cake is well-set, with a lightly browned crust. Remove from oven; cool on baking rack for 10 minutes. Invert Bundt pan to remove cake, and cool on baking rack for 30 minutes. Serve warm or cool.

Slice cake leftovers and wrap each slice individually with Saran or freezer wrap. Stack in an airtight container and store in freezer for up to 4 months. Remove and thaw slices as needed.

EGG CUSTARD

Yield: Serves 4

Ingredients:

2 eggs
2 egg yolks
2 cups milk
½ cup sugar
1 tsp. pure vanilla extract
¼ tsp. cinnamon
¼ tsp. nutmeg
2–4 cups hot water

Preheat oven to 325 degrees Fahrenheit.

In a medium saucepan over medium-low heat, add milk and bring to a simmer, stirring occasionally.

In a large mixing bowl, add eggs, egg yolks, and sugar. Whisk until fully combined. Add hot milk. Whisk rapidly until fully combined. Add vanilla, and whisk gently to incorporate. Skim foam from custard and discard.

Pour custard into four standard-size custard baking cups or ramekins. Dust the top of each cup with a sprinkle of nutmeg and cinnamon.

Transfer custard cups to a 9 x 13-inch baking pan, leaving a 2-inch space between cups. Pour hot water into the baking pan until it reaches about halfway up the side of the custard cups.

Slowly, to avoid splashing water into the custard cups, transfer baking pan to the oven. Bake for 60 minutes or until custard is fully set. Remove baking pan from oven. Remove the custard cups from the baking pan and cool on a wire rack until they are only slightly warm.

Transfer custard cups to the refrigerator and chill for 1 hour, then serve.

ROSEMARY LEMON GRANITA
Yield: Serves 4

Ingredients:
4 sprigs rosemary
¼ cup sugar
1 cup lemon juice, fresh
1 cup water

In a small saucepan, over medium heat, add water and sugar. Stir constantly until completely dissolved. Heat until liquid is hot, but not boiling. (You will have just created what is known as simple syrup.)

Reduce heat to low. Add rosemary sprigs, simmer for 10 minutes, gently stirring occasionally. Remove pan from heat. Allow liquid to cool completely. Remove sprigs and discard (compost).

In a medium-size flat-bottom glass bowl, add lemon juice and simple syrup. Stir until combined. Transfer bowl to freezer, uncovered on a flat surface.

Set a timer for 30 minutes. At 30-minute mark, remove granita from freezer, stir, and return it to freezer immediately.

Set a timer for 45 minutes. At 45-minute mark, remove granita from freezer. Use a fork to stir and scrape down the "ice" from the sides of the granita mixture. Return to freezer immediately after scraping.

Set a timer for 30 minutes. At 30-minute mark, remove granita from freezer. The mix should be nearly frozen throughout at this point. At this stage, you can create a smooth granita or a grainy one. Smooth granita is closer in consistency to sorbet; grainy is closer to Italian-style ice.

Smooth—stir mixture with a fork, scrape down sides, stir again and immediately return to the freezer.

Grainy—scrape down sides with a fork, then scrape through entire mixture. Immediately return to the freezer.

For both smooth and grainy, continue to repeat the process above every 30 minutes until mixture is frozen. Once fully frozen, the granita is ready to serve. Granita may be stored in the freezer for 1–2 days.

Additional Herb and Fruit Granita Flavor Combinations *(Swap the lemon and rosemary for one of the following flavor combinations.)*	
4 sprigs basil	1 cup pear juice
4 sprigs basil	1 cup peach juice
4 sprigs cilantro	1 cup tomato juice
4 sprigs cilantro	1 cup apple juice
4 sprigs mint	1 cup watermelon juice
4 sprigs mint	1 cup carrot juice
4 sprigs oregano	1 cup blackberry juice
4 sprigs oregano	1 cup plum juice
4 sprigs parsley	1 cup grapefruit juice
4 sprigs parsley	1 cup pineapple juice
4 sprigs thyme	1 cup grape juice
4 sprigs thyme	1 cup cherry juice

DRIED FRUIT COMPOTE
Yield: 2 cups

Ingredients:
½ cup dried apricots
½ cup dried apples
½ cup dried pears
½ cup dried peaches
¼ cup lemon juice
Water

In a medium saucepan over medium heat, add all dried fruit and lemon juice. Add water until dried fruits are all submerged. Do not fill pan with water; fill only until fruits are covered. Heat to just below boiling; gently stir regularly. Reduce heat, cover, and simmer for 20 minutes, or until fruits are tender. Remove from heat.

Stir fruits until combined; this will give you a chunky fruit compote. Optionally, process in food processor if you prefer a smooth mixture. If you prefer a sweet compote, add a little sugar and mix until fully incorporated.

Compote may be served warm or cooled and is great with scones, cookies, biscuits, potato pancakes, and crepes. May be stored in the refrigerator for up to one week or frozen in a freezer-safe container for up to 6 months.

FRESH STRAWBERRY MINT COMPOTE
Yield: 4 cups

Ingredients:
4 cups strawberries, sliced
1 cup mint leaves
½ cup sugar
1½ cups water

In a medium saucepan over medium heat, add mint, sugar, and water. Bring to a boil, stirring occasionally. Reduce heat; cover and simmer for 15 minutes. Remove mint and discard (compost). Add strawberries; simmer uncovered for 5 minutes, stirring gently. Remove from heat. Cool for 15 minutes.

Compote may be poured into a serving bowl and served or, for a smooth compote, pour mix into a food processor and puree before serving. Compote may be served warm or cooled and is great with scones, cookies, biscuits, potato pancakes, and crepes. May be stored in the refrigerator for up to one week or frozen in a freezer-safe container for up to 6 months.

BLOOD ORANGE BARS
Yield: 12–16 bars

Any citrus fruit may be substituted for the blood oranges in this recipe, but blood oranges create a great flavor twist and add a lovely pink hue to this treat.

Ingredients:

2¼ cups whole wheat pastry flour
½ cup fresh blood orange juice
⅛ cup blood orange zest
4 eggs
1 cup butter
1 cup sugar
½ cup confectioner's sugar
½ tsp. baking powder

Preheat oven to 350 degrees Fahrenheit.

In a large mixing bowl, add 2 cups of wheat flour and sugar. Cut butter into chunks and add to mixing bowl. Using a pastry cutter, cut butter into flour until fully crumbed.

Spread crust mix evenly into a greased 9 x 13-inch glass baking pan, gently pressing crust down to form a solid layer. Bake for 15 minutes or until crust is lightly browned. Remove from oven, and set aside.

In a large mixing bowl, add confectioner's sugar, eggs, blood orange juice, ¼ cup whole wheat flour, baking powder, and orange zest. Whisk together until fully combined.

Pour orange juice mixture evenly over crust. Return to oven and bake 20 minutes or until topping is set and a light crust is formed on top. Remove from oven, and cool on a baking rack until bars are room temperature. Cut into squares and serve. Optionally, a light dusting of confectioner's sugar may be sprinkled on top of the bars.

HONEY WALNUT NOUGAT

Yield: 64 1-inch square pieces

Ingredients:
1 cup honey
1 cup walnuts, chopped
½ cup sugar
2 egg whites
3 Tbsp. corn syrup
1 tsp. pure vanilla extract
½ cups water

In a large saucepan over medium-high heat, add sugar, 2 Tbsp. corn syrup, and water. Bring to a boil, stirring regularly. Boil to soft-crack stage (290 degrees Fahrenheit).

Just before sugar mixture reaches the soft-crack stage: In a large saucepan over medium-high heat, add honey and 1 Tbsp. corn syrup. Bring to a boil, stirring occasionally.

When sugar mixture reaches soft-crack stage: In a large mixing bowl, beat egg whites until stiff. If you have trouble getting egg whites to stiffen, add a pinch of salt. Gradually add sugar mixture to egg whites, continuously beating to combine.

Bring honey mixture to soft-crack stage. Gradually add honey mixture to egg-white mix, beating continuously to combine. You will now have a nougat base. Fold in nuts.

Using a double boiler, over medium heat, transfer nougat mix to top pan. Cook for 15 minutes, stirring regularly. Add vanilla, stirring regularly until nougat candy begins to dry and stiffen. Remove from heat.

Pour nougat into a greased 8 x 8-inch glass baking pan. Press nougat down until evenly distributed through pan. Cool until firm; then cut into 1-inch square pieces. Store in airtight container for up to 2 weeks.

BASIC PIECRUST RECIPE
Yield: 1 9-inch piecrust

You can purchase preformed piecrusts—but why? It's so easy and much cheaper to make one of your own, and the fresh taste beats out any processed blend every time. Many piecrust variations exist, but this basic recipe is great for use with both sweet and savory pies.

Ingredients:
1¼ cups all-purpose flour
½ cup butter, cold
¼ cup cold water
¼ tsp. salt

In a large mixing bowl, add flour and salt. Stir until fully combined. Cut butter into chunks and add to mixing bowl. Using a pastry cutter, cut butter into flour until fully crumbed. Add water, a small amount at a time, stirring continuously until the dough forms into a ball. (You may not need to use all the water, so do be sure to add it slowly and stop adding when dough ball is formed.)

Wrap the dough in plastic wrap and refrigerate for 6 hours or, ideally, overnight.

When ready for use, remove dough from refrigerator and unwrap. Transfer dough to a floured pastry sheet. Use a lightly floured rolling pin to gently flatten dough in a circular shape to fill a 9-inch pie plate.

Transfer dough circle to pie plate. Press the dough into the bottom of the pie plate, then gently shape the dough evenly across the sides, leaving a small flap over the top of the pan. Trim excess dough.

If desired, create a decorative piecrust edge. The easiest edges to make are crisscross edges or petal crust edges.

For a crisscross edge, use the tines of a fork at an angle to make fork marks around the entire crust edge. Then repeat the process holding the fork at the opposite angle to form an X pattern.

For a petal crust edge, place your finger tip to the inside of the crust edge. Then press the crust around your fingertip to form a small pocket (or fluted edge). Continue this process around the entire piecrust edge. Use the tines of a fork to gently press down and mark the center of each pocket.

If you have a lot of excess dough scraps, another fun embellishment is to use small cookie cutters or a pastry knife to cut out ½-inch shapes that can be scattered and pressed in along the piecrust edge, overlapped around the entire edge, or used on top of the pie filling to create a unique design. For example, star shapes are a nice touch for Fourth of July pies.

WILD BLACKBERRY PIE
Yield: 1 pie

Wild blackberries are native to our area of Kentucky, but any jam made with fresh blackberries will do. Each delivers a different taste, but both are simply divine!

Ingredients:
4 egg yolks
½ cup wild blackberry jam
½ cup butter
½ cup heavy cream
½ cup sugar
2 Tbsp. flour
1 9-inch piecrust shell, unbaked

Preheat oven to 350 degrees Fahrenheit.

In a large mixing bowl, add butter and sugar. Beat until fully combined and smooth.

In a small mixing bowl, whisk egg yolks until frothy.

Add eggs to butter mixture, beat until fully combined and smooth. Add jam, cream and flour, and stir until ingredients are fully incorporated.

Pour batter into 9-inch piecrust shell, distributing evenly. Bake for 45 minutes or until pie is well-set and firm in center.

EASY SWEET POTATO PIE

Yield: 1 pie

Ingredients:

2 cups baked sweet potatoes,
*   pureed*
3 eggs
1 cup sugar
½ cup butter
¼ cup evaporated milk
1 tsp. pure vanilla extract
1 tsp. nutmeg, ground
1 tsp. lemon juice
1 9-inch piecrust shell, unbaked

Preheat oven to 350 degrees Fahrenheit.

In a large mixing bowl, add pureed sweet potatoes, eggs, sugar, and butter. Beat until fully combined and smooth. Add evaporated milk, vanilla, nutmeg, and lemon juice. Beat until fully combined and smooth.

Pour batter into 9-inch piecrust shell, distributing evenly. Bake for 50 minutes or until pie is well-set and firm in center.

9. Get Wild:

Celebrating Your DIY Style

Now that you are well on your way to enjoying the fruits of your labor, a yard full of chickens, and all the substantial strides you've made toward living a more sustainable lifestyle, it's time to party!

WHAT'S YOUR CELEBRATION STYLE?

Take this mini-quiz to begin your path to selecting the best way to celebrate your eco-savvy skills with family and friends.

Circle the number of the answer that you best identify with:

What are you most excited to showcase?

1. Eggs from your lively brood.
2. Vegetables from your garden.
3. Fruits from your sweet harvest.
4. A variety of preservation skills.
5. A variety of herbs and floral delights.
6. A variety of sweet and savory dishes.

What statement describes you best?
1. Your favorite days begin with you kicking the alarm clock and sleeping in.
2. You are up bright and early tending your garden, enjoying the brilliant sunrise.
3. You live for late-night conversations and gourmet snacks.
4. You love spending a casual afternoon outdoors enjoying the onset of dusk.
5. You enjoy the predictable rhythm of your daily schedule.
6. You are most at home in the kitchen and could cook from dawn to dusk.

Which Muppet would you most like to invite to dinner?
1. The Great Gonzo and Camilla the Chicken
2. Kermit the Frog
3. Animal
4. Fozzie Bear
5. Miss Piggy
6. Swedish Chef

Scoring: Give yourself one point for each 1–6 answer. Tally up the points for each. The number with the most points is your celebration match.

1 _____ 2 _____ 3 _____ 4 _____ 5 _____ 6 _____

Mostly 1's: Carefree days, informal attire, and relaxed conversations rock your party world. A scrumptious brunch is the celebration for you!

Mostly 2's: Every day for you is Earth Day, and there's nothing you enjoy more than prepping vegetables from the garden. A garden party is exactly where you belong!

Mostly 3's: You thrive on lively conversation, savory snacks, and dancing until the wee hours of the night. A cocktail party is just what the spin doctor ordered!

Mostly 4's: Picnic benches, coolers full of refreshments, impromptu buffets, and volleyball in the sand all boost your celebratory mood. A barbecue party tingles your taste buds!

Mostly 5's: You spend hours dreaming up tablescapes, adore floral centerpieces, and clamor for a fresh cup of tea to dunk your biscuits in. An elegant tea party is your ideal refined celebration.

Mostly 6's: Heaping plates full of food, formal place settings, and clever culinary combinations leave you itchin' to get into the kitchen. A four-course sit-down dinner party is a celebration you'll truly enjoy hosting!

WHAT IF MY NUMBERS DON'T MATCH UP?

If you wound up with a split number preference, such as two tallies in the number 2 and one tally in the number 4 slot, you can certainly join your interests and host a tea and barbecue bash!

If your numbers are all over the spectrum or you just couldn't choose just one answer, no worries: you are simply a party gal who loves a great celebration no matter what the venue!

YOU'RE INVITED...TO A BRUNCH CELEBRATION

Sample Menu
Brown Bread Breakfast Soufflé (page 153)
Creamy Chicken Bake (page 172)
Cheddar Deviled Eggs
Grandma Jo's Orange Carrot Bread (page 202)
Banana Nut Muffins (pages 208–209)
Dried Fruit Compote (page 218)
Assorted fresh juices
Coffees and teas
Fresh fruit, crudités, maple syrup

CHEDDAR DEVILED EGGS

Yield: Serves 10–12

Ingredients:
6 eggs, hard-boiled and peeled
1 cup sharp cheddar cheese,
   finely grated
¼ cup mayonnaise
1 Tbsp. onion, minced
1 tsp. stone-ground mustard
Salt and pepper

Cut eggs in half, vertically. Remove yolks from whites. Set whites aside.

In a medium mixing bowl, add egg yolks, cheddar, mayonnaise, onion, and mustard. Mix until all ingredients are fully incorporated and mix is smooth. Stuff egg whites with deviled egg mixture and set them on a tray, egg white side down. Chill for 1 hour, then serve.

YOU'RE INVITED...TO A GARDEN PARTY CELEBRATION

Sample Menu
  Garden Chicken Cacciatore (page 162)
  Roasted Cauliflower (page 182)
  Cucumber and Green Bean Salad (page 183)
  Garden Vegetable Dip
  Basil Spinach Dip
  Brown bread wedges and crudités
  Assorted fresh juices
  Coffees and teas
  Dessert: Rosemary Lemon Granita (page 216)

GARDEN VEGETABLE DIP

Yield: Serves 6-8

Ingredients:

1 carrot, chopped
1 red bell pepper, seeded and
chopped
½ cup onion, chopped
½ cup broccoli, chopped
1 cup mayonnaise
½ cup mild cheddar cheese,
grated fine
2 Tbsp. fresh parsley
2 Tbsp. vinegar
½ tsp. curry powder
½ tsp. salt
½ tsp. pepper

Using a food processor, add carrots, pepper, onion, broccoli, and parsley. Pulse until chopped fine and mixed. Add curry powder, vinegar, salt, and pepper. Pulse until fully combined and smooth.

In a medium mixing bowl, add vegetable mix, cheese, and mayonnaise. Stir until thoroughly combined. Transfer dip to a dip bowl and chill for 1 hour. Serve with crudités or crackers.

BASIL SPINACH DIP

Yield: Serves 10–12

Ingredients:

1 cup spinach leaves
1 cup basil
1 cup Parmesan cheese, grated
8 oz. cream cheese
½ cup soft goat cheese
1 clove garlic, minced
2 Tbsp. olive oil

Using a food processor, add spinach, basil, and garlic. Pulse until fully chopped. Add oil and Parmesan; pulse until fully mixed and smooth.

In a medium mixing bowl, add spinach mixture, cream cheese, and goat cheese, and stir until fully combined. Transfer dip to a serving bowl. Cover and refrigerate for 4 hours. Serve with crudités, crackers, or bread.

YOU'RE INVITED...TO A COCKTAIL PARTY CELEBRATION

Sample Menu
Eggplant Dip (page 184)
Fresh Guacamole Dip
Asparagus Rolls
Stuffed Mushrooms
Garden Herb Cheese Ball
Sustainable Garden Chicken Meatballs
Wine Biscuits (page 205)
Blackberry Wine Jelly (page 110)
Brown bread wedges, assorted chips and crudités
Garden-Fresh Bloody Mary
Assorted beverages

ASPARAGUS ROLLS

Yield: Serves 12–15

Ingredients:
2 cups asparagus spears, cooked,
drained and cooled
1 cup cream cheese
1 loaf Brown Bread (page 200)
4 Tbsp. sour cream
½ tsp. fresh dill, chopped thin
¼ tsp. pepper, ground
4 Tbsp. olive oil

Preheat oven to 350 degrees Fahrenheit.

Slice brown bread into thin slices (about ⅛-inch thick). Remove crust edge. Flatten each slice of bread with a rolling pin.

In a medium mixing bowl, add cream cheese, sour cream, dill, and pepper; stir until fully combined. Smear a bit of the cream cheese mixture on each slice of flattened bread. Place an asparagus spear on the edge of each slice of bread. Roll the bread, keeping the asparagus spear in the center of the roll.

Transfer asparagus rolls to a greased cookie sheet, seam side down. Using a basting brush, brush melted butter on the top of each roll. Bake for 15 minutes or until lightly browned. Remove from oven; cool sheets on a wire baking rack for 10 minutes. Slice asparagus rolls in thirds and arrange on a serving tray. (If the rolls are finicky about staying closed, use a toothpick for each to secure the ends.)

Chick Tip: Save brown bread crust edges to make bread crumbs. Leave them out over night to stale, crumble, and store in an airtight container for future use.

STUFFED MUSHROOMS

Yield: Serves 12–15

Ingredients:

24 white button mushroom caps
24 white button mushroom stems, minced
¼ cup bacon, cooked and crumbled
½ cup tomato, diced
1 cup croutons, crushed
1 cup mozzarella cheese, grated
¼ cup Parmesan cheese, grated
2 Tbsp. fresh parsley, minced
1 Tbsp. fresh oregano, minced
2 Tbsp. olive oil

Preheat oven to 425 degrees Fahrenheit.

Heat oil in a medium cast iron skillet over medium heat. Add mushroom stems, and sauté until soft and lightly browned. Remove from heat. Stir in bacon, tomato, croutons, mozzarella, and Parmesan.

Stuff mushroom caps with stuffing mixture, packing firmly and making a rounded mound atop the mushroom cap. Place mushroom caps in a greased 10 x 14-inch glass baking dish, mushroom side down. Bake for 15 minutes or until mushrooms are soft and stuffing is lightly browned. Remove from oven, transfer to a platter, and serve.

GARDEN HERB CHEESE BALL

Yield: Serves 8-10

Ingredients:

8 oz. cream cheese
½ cup sharp cheddar cheese, grated
½ cup bleu cheese, crumbled
1 Tbsp. fresh parsley, chopped fine
1 Tbsp. fresh rosemary, chopped fine
1 Tbsp. fresh oregano, chopped fine
½ cup pecans, chopped

In a large mixing bowl, add cream cheese, cheddar, bleu cheese, parsley, rosemary, and oregano. Stir until fully combined and smooth. Gently shape cheese mixture into a ball shape. Roll cheese ball in chopped pecans until ball is fully coated. Wrap cheese ball in wax paper, refrigerate for 4 hours. Serve with crackers.

FRESH GUACAMOLE DIP

Yield: Serves 6-8

Ingredients:

1 cup avocado, mashed
½ cup tomato, chopped
¼ cup green onions, chopped
¼ cup salsa (hot or mild, depending on preference)
1 clove garlic, minced
1 tsp. lime juice

In a medium mixing bowl, combine all ingredients, mix until smooth. Transfer to a serving bowl and serve with tortilla chips.

SUSTAINABLE GARDEN CHICKEN MEATBALLS

Yield: Serves 10–12

Ingredients:

2 lbs. chicken, ground

2 eggs

2 cups tomatoes, peeled and
*   chopped*

½ cup tomato paste

½ cup rolled oats

½ cup Parmesan cheese

1 clove of garlic, minced

1 Tbsp. fresh oregano, chopped
*   fine*

1 Tbsp. fresh basil, chopped fine

1 Tbsp. fresh parsley, chopped
*   fine*

2 Tbsp. olive oil

In a large mixing bowl, add ground chicken, rolled oats, parsley, eggs, and Parmesan cheese. Mix by hand until all ingredients are fully combined. Shape chicken mixture into 1-inch round meatball shapes.

In a medium mixing bowl, add tomatoes, tomato paste, garlic, oregano, and basil. Stir gently until thoroughly mixed.

Heat olive oil in a large cast iron skillet over medium heat. Add chicken meatballs to skillet. Cook meatballs, turning frequently until all sides are browned. Reduce heat to medium-low. Pour tomato sauce over meatballs and simmer for 30 minutes. Remove from heat. Transfer meatballs to a serving tray. Pour remaining sauce in skillet over meatballs. Serve warm.

GARDEN-FRESH BLOODY MARY

Yield: Serves 6-8

Ingredients:
6 cups tomato juice
⅓ cup lemon juice
1 cup vodka
¼ cup Worcestershire sauce
1 Tbsp. hot sauce
1 Tbsp. black pepper, ground
2 tsp. cayenne pepper, ground
½ tsp. celery salt
Celery stalks

In a gallon-size pitcher, add all ingredients, and stir until fully combined. Serve in glasses filled with ice. Garnish with celery stalk.

YOU'RE INVITED...TO A BARBECUE PARTY CELEBRATION

Sample Menu
Cilantro Black Bean Dip
Guinness Beer Can Chicken (page 131)
Barbecue Lima Beans (page 188)
Herb Garden Radishes (page 190)
Cheddar Herb Muffins (pages 209–210)
Fresh corn on the cob, grilled
Assorted chips and crudités
Assorted beverages
Dessert: Drunken Fruit Whipped Pie (page 117)

CILANTRO BLACK BEAN DIP

Yield: Serves 6-8

Ingredients:
*2 cups black beans, cooked and
    drained*
*1 cup Monterey Jack cheese,
    grated*
1 onion, diced
¼ cup fresh cilantro
Salt and pepper

Preheat oven to 375 degrees Fahrenheit.

Using a food processor, add beans, onion, cilantro, and a pinch of pepper and salt. Pulse until fully mixed and smooth.

Transfer dip to a small (4-cup) baking dish. Top dip with cheese. Bake for 10–15 minutes or until cheese is lightly browned and bubbling. Remove from oven and serve warm with tortilla chips.

YOU'RE INVITED...TO A DINNER PARTY CELEBRATION

Sample Menu

Starter
Easy Artichoke Dip
Brown bread wedges

First Course
Stuffed Carrot Soup (page 181)

Second Course
Black Walnut Butternut Chicken (page 164)
Baked Brussels Sprouts (page 180)

Dessert
Basic Irish Scones (page 211)
Fresh Strawberry Mint Compote (page 219)
Whipped cream

Assorted beverages

EASY ARTICHOKE DIP

Yield: Serves 10–12

Ingredients:

2 cups artichoke hearts, chopped

*1 cup mozzarella cheese,
    shredded*

*1 cup Parmesan cheese,
    shredded*

1 Tbsp. garlic, minced

1 cup mayonnaise

1 Tbsp. fresh parsley, minced

Preheat oven to 350 degrees Fahrenheit.

In a large mixing bowl, add all ingredients and stir until fully combined. Pour ingredients into a 9 x 13-inch glass baking pan and spread evenly. Bake for 25 minutes. Remove from oven, and serve with tortilla chips or wedges of Brown Bread (page 200).

YOU'RE INVITED...TO A TEA PARTY CELEBRATION

Sample Menu
> Two-Minute Fruit Dip
> Strawberry Raspberry Kiwi Dip
> Scotch Chicken Eggs (page 151)
> Rolled Oat Cakes with Blackberry Bourbon Sauce (page 206)
> Sweet Scones (page 212)
> Pear Basil Preserves (page 110)
> Fresh Herbal Teas
> Fresh fruits and crackers

TWO-MINUTE FRUIT DIP

Yield: Serves 8–10

Ingredients:
1 cup strawberries, pureed
1 banana, mashed
8 oz. cream cheese
¼ cup brown sugar

In a medium mixing bowl, whip all ingredients until fully combined and smooth. Transfer to a serving bowl and serve with fruits for dipping (sliced apples, sliced pears, strawberries, grapes, cantaloupe spears, etc.) or vanilla wafers.

STRAWBERRY RASPBERRY KIWI DIP

Yield: Serves 8 -10

Ingredients:

½ cup strawberries, capped and
  chopped
¼ cup raspberries
¼ cup kiwi, peeled and chopped
½ cup sour cream
½ tsp. pure vanilla extract

Using a blender or food processor, add all ingredients and pulse until pureed and fully combined. Transfer to a serving bowl and serve with fruits for dipping (sliced apples, sliced pears, strawberries, grapes, cantaloupe spears, etc.) or vanilla wafers.

ABC'S OF HERBAL TEAS

Brewed from ingredients like cinnamon, mint, raspberry leaves, sage, lemon balm, and chamomile, herbal teas are not true teas and don't always contain an herb. The classification "herbal tea" is simply used for teas that do not contain any part of the *camellia sinensis,* the plant traditional tea leaves are harvested from.

Why do people love herbal teas? Exceptional flavor and caffeine-free properties are two desirable attractions, but many herbal teas also offer attractive natural remedy properties. For example, mint is a known digestive aid, chamomile is often used as a sleep aid, lavender may calm nerves, lemon verbena may help aid congestion, and rosemary is often used to help stimulate circulation.

When using fresh ingredients for tea making, it's best to pick them directly prior to brewing the tea. Rinse herbs or flowers to rid them of dust and dirt, then crush leaves or petals gently with your fingertips to help release their oils before placing in your mesh tea strainer or tea bag.

DO NOT use herbs, flowers, or fruits that have been sprayed with fertilizer, pesticides, or any other chemical. Even when washed, they may contain trace toxins that are not ideal for your overall health and well-being.

DO be mindful of allergies. If you do not have experience with an ingredient, proceed with caution. If you have known allergies or suspect you may have allergies to certain herbs or plants, always consult a physician prior to consumption.

For brewing tea, always use water that has been purified. Trace minerals and elements of well water, or water that has not been purified first, can and likely will affect the end result of the tea, sometimes adding a bitter taste. Purified water allows the fruit, flower, or herb flavors in your tea to shine.

An ancient remedy that is still in practice today to help curb plant allergies, including hay fever, is to consume a teaspoon of local honey every day. Whether it works or not, honey is a great sweetener for your daily tea, so it's a win-win either way!

HERBAL TEA COMPANIONS

Pair the ingredient from the first column with the complementary ingredient in the last column to create a delicious herbal tea blend

½ tsp. cinnamon	+	½ tsp. cloves, dried and ground
1 Tbsp. diced lemon peel	+	1 Tbsp. dried lavender flowers
1 Tbsp. diced orange peel	+	1 Tbsp. fresh mint leaves
1 Tbsp. diced orange peel	+	1 tsp. ground cloves
1 Tbsp. dried blueberries	+	1 Tbsp. dried blackberries
1 Tbsp. dried chamomile flowers	+	1 tsp. dried hibiscus petals
1 Tbsp. dried chamomile flowers	+	1 Tbsp. fresh lemon verbena
1 Tbsp. dried lavender flowers	+	1 Tbsp. dried chamomile flowers
1 Tbsp. dried raspberries	+	1 Tbsp. fresh sage
1 Tbsp. fresh mint leaves	+	1 tsp. marigold petals
1 Tbsp. fresh mint leaves	+	1 Tbsp. fresh peppermint leaves
1 Tbsp. fresh rosemary	+	1 Tbsp. fresh sage
1 Tbsp. fresh sage	+	1 Tbsp. dried chamomile flowers
1 Tbsp. fresh sage	+	1 Tbsp. fresh lemon verbena
1 tsp. crushed anise seed	+	1 Tbsp. fresh peppermint
1 tsp. dried alfalfa leaves, crushed	+	1 Tbsp. fresh sage
1 tsp. dried celery leaves	+	1 Tbsp. fresh parsley leaves
2 dried apple rings	+	1 tsp. cinnamon
4 fresh rose petals	+	1 Tbsp. fresh mint leaves

For hot herb tea: Pour hot water over desired herb combination; steep 5 to 10 minutes (depending upon preferred strength of tea).

For iced herb tea: In a small saucepan, over medium-high heat, add 2 cups of water and desired herb combination. Bring to a boil, reduce heat, and simmer for 20 minutes. Remove from heat, cool and strain, reserving liquid. Mix tea liquid with 4 cups of water and ice. Serve.

For sun herb tea: Fill a sun tea container with 1 gallon of water and desired herb combination. Steep in full sun for 6–12 hours. Strain and serve with ice.

YOU'RE INVITED...TO A HOLIDAY CELEBRATION

All the parties featured can easily be used for holiday celebrations, but, for major holidays such as Thanksgiving and Christmas, special treats like egg nog add a festive touch. Try adding some of these favorites to your menu during the holiday season.

MULLED RED WINE

Yield: Serves 4- 6

Super simple to make, but a real winter warmer-upper that's always well received at winter holiday celebrations.

Ingredients:

1 quart wine

2 cinnamon sticks

¼ cup lemon peel, grated

¼ cup orange peel, grated

¼ cup cranberries

4 clove leaves

½ cup sugar

In a large saucepan, over medium heat, heat all ingredients until warm. Remove from heat, strain, and serve. If you prefer wine at room temperature, strain and allow wine to sit until it cools. If you prefer a stronger mulled wine, allow wine to sit for 1 hour before straining. Serve at room temperature or gently reheat if you would like to serve the wine warm.

HOT SORGHUM CIDER

Yield: Serves 4-6

Wonderful for fall holiday celebrations or autumn barbecues.

Ingredients:

*4 cups fresh apple juice (or
    unsweetened organic apple
    juice)*
¼ cup lemon juice
6 cloves, whole
2 cinnamon sticks
¼ cup sorghum

In a large saucepan over medium-high heat, add apple juice and sorghum. Stir until fully combined. Add cinnamon sticks and cloves; bring to a boil. Reduce heat to low, simmer for 10 minutes. Add lemon juice, stir until fully incorporated. Simmer for 5 minutes. Remove from heat. Remove cinnamon sticks and cloves, and discard. Serve hot or slightly cooled.

CLASSIC EGG NOG
Yield: Serves 4-6

If I'm not serving fresh egg nog, it somehow feels like the Christmas holidays are incomplete. This is not your store-brand egg nog, though, and even friends who claim to not like egg nog will love this fresh treat.

Ingredients:
3 fresh egg yolks
3 fresh egg whites
3 cups milk
1 cup sugar
1 cup heavy cream
½ cup whiskey
Nutmeg, ground

In a large mixing bowl, add egg yolks, and beat lightly for 1 minute. Gradually add ¾ cup of sugar, continuously beating eggs until sugar is fully incorporated. Add milk and cream, and beat for 1 minute.

In a double boiler, add egg mixture to top pan. Heat until mixture thickens, stirring regularly. Add ¼ cup whiskey. Heat until mixture rethickens, stirring regularly. Remove from heat. Cool to room temperature. Add remaining whiskey, and stir until whiskey is incorporated. Transfer to refrigerator, and chill for 2 hours.

In a large mixing bowl, add egg whites and beat until stiff peaks are formed. Gradually add ¼ cup sugar, beating until stiff peaks are re-formed. Fold chilled egg whiskey mix into egg whites. Pour mix into a punch bowl, sprinkle with nutmeg, and serve.

SPICED MILK

Yield: Serves 2-4

Inspired by Cinco de Mayo celebrations, this delicious treat is refreshing all year round. Serve it chilled in the summer and warm in the winter.

Ingredients:

4 cups milk
1-inch slice of ginger root
2 cinnamon sticks
1 vanilla bean
10 cardamom seeds, lightly
crushed
6 cloves

In a medium saucepan over low heat, add all ingredients. Simmer for 10 minutes. Increase heat to medium, and heat until steaming. Remove from heat, cover and set on a trivet to steep for 45 minutes.

Strain milk; discard spices. Chill milk in refrigerator for 1 hour, then serve. If you prefer warm milk, reheat over low heat.

CHOCOLATE ORANGE TORTE
Yield: Serves 10-12

Superbly rich, this torte will put the "wow" in any holiday celebration. For a fun twist, use it as an alternative to traditional birthday cake.

Ingredients:

1 cup semisweet chocolate,
*   chopped*
1½ cups pecans, chopped fine
½ cup sugar
½ cup Cabernet Sauvignon (any)
6 egg whites
6 egg yolks
Orange Tangerine Marmalade
*   (page 114)*
Whipped cream
Cocoa powder

Preheat oven to 375 degrees Fahrenheit.

In a large saucepan, over medium heat, add pecans, sugar, wine, and chocolate. Stir regularly until chocolate is fully melted and all ingredients are fully combined. Remove from heat. Set aside on baking rack to cool.

In a small mixing bowl, beat egg whites until peaks are formed. In a separate small mixing bowl, beat egg yolks until smooth. Add egg yolks to cooled chocolate mix, and stir until fully combined. Add egg whites to cooled chocolate mix; stir gently until fully folded into mix.

Divide batter in half and pour evenly into two nonstick (or greased) 8 x 8-inch baking pans. Transfer pans to oven and bake for 50 minutes or until center is fully set. Remove from oven, and cool on a baking rack for 15 minutes.

Remove first cake layer from pan and set on a serving tray. Spread a ¼-inch layer of marmalade evenly across the top of the torte layer. Remove second cake layer from pan and set layer atop the marmalade layer. Transfer torte to refrigerator to chill for one hour.

Remove torte from refrigerator. Top with whipped cream. Sprinkle cocoa powder lightly atop whipped cream. Slice and serve.

YOU'RE INVITED...TO GIRLS' NIGHT OUT

Until now, we've mainly used our garden powers for home and hearth, but nature's bounty also offers a wealth of beauty benefits. Invite your friends over for a spa night or try one of these of luxurious treatments before you step out on the town. All are created straight from your kitchen!

EGG-WHITE MASK

Cleans impurities from pores of all skin types.

In a small bowl, whisk one egg white. Spread egg white over face in a thick layer, avoiding eye area, mouth and nose openings. Allow egg to dry completely, then wash off with warm water.

HONEY LEMON ROSEMARY MASK

First-class pampering for normal-to-oily skin.

Ingredients:
2 Tbsp. honey
1 tsp. lemon juice
1 tsp. fresh rosemary, minced

In a small bowl, mix all ingredients. Warm in microwave for 10–15 seconds (should be warm, but not hot to the touch). Spread on face in a thin layer, avoiding eye area, mouth, and nose openings. Leave on for 30 minutes, then wash off with warm water.

SEA SALT OATMEAL MASK

This a gentle softener and clarifier for all skin types.

2 Tbsp. ground oats
2 Tbsp. olive oil
¼ tsp. sea salt

In a small bowl, add oats and sea salt. Stir until fully combined. Add olive oil, and stir until fully mixed.

Spread on face in a thin layer, avoiding eye area, mouth, and nose openings. Leave on for 15 minutes, then wash off with warm water.

RELAXING HERB FACIAL

A stress reliever and skin soother for all skin types.

Wet a towel with warm tea: chamomile, rosemary, or peppermint are good choices. Lay towel over face, keeping eyes closed. Allow to soak in until towel begins to cool. Remove towel. Rinse face with warm water, if desired.

CHAMOMILE HAIR BRIGHTENER

Gives all hair types a boost of shine.

Ingredients:
2 Tbsp. chamomile flower heads
2 cups water

In a small saucepan over medium-high heat, add water and flower heads. Bring to a boil. Boil for 1 minute. Remove from heat and cool for 10 minutes. Strain chamomile from water, reserving water. Allow water to cool to room temperature. Rinse clean hair with chamomile water. Air-dry hair and style as usual.

HONEY SUGAR SHOWER SCRUB

Sweet scrub to moisturize and exfoliate all skin types.

Ingredients:
1 Tbsp. raw honey
2 Tbsp. raw sugar
2 Tbsp. olive oil

In a small bowl, add all ingredients; stir until fully combined. Shower as usual, then scoop mixture into hands and gently rub into skin, paying particular attention to rough spots like elbows, knees, and heels. Rinse thoroughly. Dry off after shower as you normally would and admire your soft, well-exfoliated skin.

ALOE GEL FOR SUNBURN RELIEF

Select an older (lower) leaf from your aloe plant. Snip 4 inches from the top of the leaf. Slice the leaf open lengthwise and scoop out the gel into a small bowl. Using fingertips, apply gel gently in a thick layer over sun-affected skin. Allow gel to air-dry completely. Reapply as needed.

YOU'RE INVITED...TO HAVE SOME DIY FUN

Think of the gifts you best remember receiving. Chances are they were hand-crafted or personalized in some way by the giver. In addition to showcasing your wonderful bounty, showcase your unique talents with hand-crafted embellishments or gifts at your next celebration.

SALT DOUGH ORNAMENTS

This recipe is terrific for year-round use. Make ornament trees for Easter, gift the ornaments at Christmas, or simply use the dough to create personalized wall hangings or to fashion napkin holders.

Ingredients:
1 cup salt
4 cups flour
1½ cups water

Preheat oven to 225 degrees Fahrenheit.

In a large mixing bowl, combine all ingredients. Knead until a smooth dough is achieved.

Transfer dough to a lightly floured, clean work surface. Use a rolling pin to flatten and spread dough to a ½-inch thickness. Use cookie cutters, molds, or a butter knife to cut shapes from the dough.

Use a straw or a toothpick to form a hole (about ½-inch from the top of the ornament) to later thread an ornament hanger or ribbon through. Transfer dough shapes to cookie sheets.

Bake for 25–30 minutes or until fully baked. Remove cookies from oven. Transfer to a baker's rack and cool completely.

Use water paints, acrylic paints, craft glue, permanent markers, glitter, and other embellishments to decorate.

CANDIED HERBS AND FLOWERS

Perfect for decorating cakes, cupcakes, brownies, and drinks, or for use as plate garnishes. Popular selections are mint leaves, rose petals, lilacs, and violets.

Ingredients:

½ cup mint leaves
1 egg white
¼ tsp. pure vanilla extract
1 cup caster sugar

Preheat oven to 200 degrees Fahrenheit.

In a small bowl, whisk egg white with vanilla extract until fully combined. Pour sugar into a separate small bowl. Dredge mint leaves in egg. Gently dredge in sugar until fully coated. Place sugared mint leaves on a cookie sheet. Place in oven for 2–3 hours. Leave oven door slightly open for air circulation. When leaves are completely dried, remove. Cool completely prior to use.

Optionally, if you own a dehydrator, sugared mint leaves may be dried at a 110-degree setting until fully dried (about 4 hours).

DIY T-SHIRT BAG

A terrific way to recycle older T-shirts and a unique accessory to use for all types of shopping and travel purposes. This is a great craft project for birthday parties and garden clubs.

Turn T-shirt inside out. Cut off sleeves, leaving at least a 1-inch panel of fabric from the neck hole to the point where the sleeve is removed. This section will form the handles of the bag. If the neckline is narrow, you may also wish to trim around the neck opening to widen.

With the T-shirt still inside out, sew the bottom of the t-shirt sides together with tight cross stitches using a strong thread. Fish string is excellent for this purpose.

Turn the T-shirt right-side-out and voilà! You now have a simple carrying bag that can easily be folded and tucked into your pocket or purse.

If desired, reinforce the straps of the bag by stitching along the outer ends or stitching a length of ribbon across the handle area. Embellish the bag with buttons, ribbons, pins, old earrings, or other fun items to create a truly one-of-a-kind piece.

ESSENTIAL OILS AIR FRESHENER

Get your house party-ready by freshening things up nature's way.

Needed:

16 oz. clean spray bottle
   Purified or distilled water
Preferred essential oils
   (Lavender, orange, pepper-
   mint, etc.)

Fill the spray bottle with water to approximately 1 inch from the top. Add 10 drops of essential oil. Cap bottle and shake for 30 seconds. Spritz a little where needed and enjoy the lovely toxin-free scent. Be sure to shake the bottle before each use for the best results.

EGGSHELL CHALK

Adults and children alike enjoy coloring with chalk. Use this recipe to create fun party favors or to leave out during a summer party for some artistic fun in the sun.

Ingredients:
6 eggshells, emptied, washed
and dried
1 tsp. all-purpose flour
1 tsp. hot water
Natural food coloring

In a small mixing bowl, crush and grind eggshells until fully powdered. A mortar and pestle is ideal for this process.

In a separate small mixing bowl, add flour and water. Stir until mixed. Add 1 Tbsp. powdered eggshell, stir until fully mixed. This is the base for white chalk.

For colored chalk, add natural food coloring, 1 drop (or small dash) at a time until desired color is achieved (no more than 4 or 5 liquid drops, though, or else mix will become runny and will not set well).

Mold chalk into desired shape. Place shapes on a cookie tray lined with wax paper. Set tray aside in a dry, cool, dark spot. Allow chalk shapes to dry for 4 days, turning shapes over once per day.

When chalk shape is fully dry, it is ready for use.

NATURAL FOOD COLORING

Your garden is bursting with color and, with a little know-how, it's easy to utilize these colors in baking and crafts. Natural food coloring will create a more subtle hue than synthetic food colorings in addition to avoiding chemicals or questionable ingredients, that's part of the charm!

PS: If you mix a few drops with a tablespoon of vinegar and a cup of hot water, you can easily create a natural Easter egg dye from these selections as well.

Ingredients:

Red/Pink: Beets, juiced
Rhubarb, juiced
Cranberries, juiced
Raspberries, juiced and strained
Red bell peppers, seeded and juiced

Blue: Blueberries, juiced
Cornflowers, ground

Green: Spinach, juiced
Kale, juiced
Green bell peppers, seeded and juiced
Parsley, juiced

Yellow/Orange: Pineapple, juiced
Yellow bell peppers, seeded and juiced
Carrots, juiced
Paprika, ground

Purple: Purple grapes, juiced
Blackberries, juiced and strained

Brown: Cinnamon, ground
Coffee beans, finely ground

MASON JAR PARTY FAVORS AND GIFTS

Invented in the mid-1800's for food preservation, Mason jars have a pure simplicity and appealing design that have made them not only a household treasure but a craft and décor favorite.

For parties, use Mason jars as drink cups, wine glasses, utensil holders, condiment holders, napkin holders, vases, candle holders, lanterns, and for offering candies and mints.

For party favors, fill them with trinkets or a sampling of the night's menu, such as a pint of Baby Watermelon Pickles, for guests to take home. Just tie a little ribbon or raffia around the rim and attach a label or tag to dress up the jar.

Theme trinkets by season, for example:

Summer-Ready	Lip balm, mini nail polish, nail files, travel-size sunscreen, and hand sanitizer
Winter-Ready	Pocket gloves, lip balm, and hand cream

Or use the party theme to inspire you:

Barbecue	Wet wipes, candles, glow sticks, and an inflatable beach ball
Garden Party	Gardening gloves, seed packets, and gardener's soap

For holiday gifts, fill them with dried Herbal Teas (pages 241–242), Honey Sugar Shower Scrub (page 250), or soup. Any one of your canned, alcohol canned, pickled, or dried goods will surely be well-received too.

Use a single item or a combination of items. Whatever fun item you decide to fill them with or however you decide to decorate the Mason jar, guests will love the personal touch. Use this list for ideas and inspiration:

FILL MASON JARS WITH...

Bath Bombs (page 259)

Dish cloths

Makeup sponges

Sewing items

Bird seed

Dried flowers

Muffins

Shot glasses

Brownies

Dried fruits

Nuts

Soaps

Bubbles

Drink stirrers

Office supplies

Socks

Candies

Eggshell Chalk (page 255)

Ornaments

Spa items

Candles

First-aid kit

Popcorn

Stickers

Cookie cutters

Fudge

Reusable ice cubes

Toys

Cookies

Gumballs

School supplies

Trail mix

Craft supplies

Jerky

Seashells

Travel-size toiletries

BATH BOMBS

Ingredients:

1 cup baking soda

1 cup cornstarch

½ cup powdered citric acid

6 drops of essential oils

Water

In a large mixing bowl, add baking soda, cornstarch, and citric acid. Stir gently to combine. Break up any lumps until mixture is completely smooth.

Add one drop of essential oil; stir mixture. Add another drop and stir. Repeat until you have added all the drops. If you are using a weak oil scent, add up to four additional drops, stirring mix after each drop is added. If you are using a strong oil scent, reduce the amount of drops added accordingly.

Add ¼ tsp. of water to mix, and stir until fully incorporated. Continue adding water ¼ tsp. at a time, stirring in until mix is crumbly and sticks together when pinched. Do not be tempted to over-water the mix; it should still feel relatively dry to the touch.

Line a cookie sheet or flat surface with wax paper. Take a scoop of bath bomb mixture and gently roll it into a ball shape. Place the ball shape on the wax paper. Continue process until all the mix is used.

Alternatively, use a small melon scoop to form the balls, or press scoops of mixture into small silicone molds to form different shapes.

Set bath bombs aside in a cool, dry spot for 48 hours. (Note: If you live in an area with high humidity, the bath bombs may require an additional day or two of drying time.)

Store bath bombs in an airtight container in a cool, dry space for up to six months.

If you wish to color your bath bombs, the best colorant is a natural powder created from dehydrated fruits, vegetables, or flowers. Simply dehydrate the fruit, vegetable, or flower completely, then crush into powered form. Add a teaspoon of powder to the dry mix prior to adding essential oils. Use the same produce recommended in the Eggshell Chalk recipe (page 255) to achieve the color you desire.

10. Get Real:
Assessing Your
Sexy Sustainable Lifestyle

I like it when a flower or a little tuft of grass grows through a crack in the concrete. It's so fuckin' heroic.
—George Carlin

I truly envy people who seem to have everything in their lives in perfect balance.

I am not one of these people.

Hourly, I struggle to find my equilibrium, to juggle all the roles I've been blessed with—mother, wife, daughter, blogger, writer, housekeeper, volunteer, animal caretaker, sci-fi fan...

Daily, I struggle to avoid eating the entire pan of brownies I baked, to help the kids with their mounds of homework, to carve out time for exercise, to find ten seconds for a shower, to avoid mental meltdowns from work overload, and to figure out what the heck to do with my frizzy, out-of-control hair (no amount of eco-friendly anything is going to help!).

Equally challenging is finding ways to break through the noise—cell phones, television, traffic, fast food, shopping malls, and planning family vacations to Disney World. All these things primarily distract from rather than enhance sustainable-living efforts.

One of the things I asked myself before writing this book was: How do I break through the noise? How do I overcome the bubble of buzz in the world to help others carve out their own little spot of Eden? How can I possibly preach about homestead Zen when my own life often feels unbalanced?

Then I stopped a moment to breathe and quiet the noise.

I looked around.

I spied on the chickens as they pecked their merry way across my front yard.

Marveled at the plump strawberries ripening in the raised beds my husband built.

Gazed lovingly at the rows of full Mason jars and the braids of garlic in my pantry.

Watched my son open a jar of homemade applesauce and grab a fresh piece of brown bread for an after-school snack.

Smiled as my youngest son chucked his orange peels in the compost bin.

Steeped myself a cup of fresh lemon mint tea.

And it finally sank in, as I thought to myself, "We got this."

No matter what our schedule may look like or what role I play in this crazy-busy-hectic world, we are filling our days with organic goods and integrating life-giving habits for the betterment of our family and the world.

Every moment, we are breaking through the noise, creating the best possible balance between sustainable living and our industrial-laden lives.

Eden is all around me, infused into every second of my day, and that certainly makes every iota of effort worthwhile.

In a world of land versus people, where we are slowly running out of resources to sustain the population on the planet, we have to seek out and incorporate this balance.

We'll still be juggling our ever-increasing workloads. We'll still be fighting frizzy hair and checking our cell phones to find out who is having a better day on Facebook than we are.

But, despite the noise, we can break through to be stewards of the Earth and creators of more eco-friendly environments.

We can be fun, fearless, chic designers, paving a new path in what it means to be a sustainable-living pioneer.

That, my friend, is the epitome of sexy.

Remember what we discussed in the beginning?

There are four simple rules that govern this guide, and they all ring true through each page straight into very real and sometimes harried lives:

1. Baby chicks are crazy-huggable-adorable, and they grow up to be beautiful, bountiful chickens.
2. Everything fresh and organic looks, tastes, and *is* better for you.
3. Conserving our natural resources is vital to the future of our planet and better for our pocketbooks.
4. Sexy doesn't come from a bottle or a well-fitted brassiere. It radiates from inside and illuminates the world through our actions and choices.

In our nutty, cluttered world, my sincerest hope is that I have managed to interrupt the noise in your life long enough to deliver invigorating new ways for you to carve out your own little slice of nature's paradise.

When daylight floods the morning fields or sunset beckons the chickens to roost, be sure to stop, breathe, and soak it all in.

This is your fabulous sustainable-living-infused life.

This is your Eden.

Relax and enjoy!

Recipe and Instruction Index

ABC's of Herbal Teas 241

Alcohol Canning: The Forgotten Process 114

Aloe Gel for Sunburn Relief 250

Applesauce Bread 203

Asparagus Au Gratin 178

Asparagus Rolls 231

Autumn Dutch Oven-Roasted Chicken 168

Autumn Vegetable Salad 196

Baby Pickled Watermelon 125

Baked Brussels Sprouts 180

Barbecue Lima Beans 188

Basic Dry Brine for Chicken 130

Basic Fruit Leather Recipe 135

Basic Irish Scone Recipe 211

Basic Muffin Recipe 208

Basic Piecrust Recipe 222

Basic Wet Brine for Chicken 129

Basil Spinach Dip 230

Bath Bombs 259

Birds in a Brown Bread Nest 156

Blackberry Beet Soup 179

Blackberry Bourbon Sauce 207

Blackberry Wine Jelly 110

Black Walnut Butternut Chicken 164

Blanching 101 102

Blood Orange Bars 220

Boiling-Water Canning Method 107

Brown Bread 200

Brown Bread Breakfast Soufflé 153

Brown Bread Crumbs 201

Can I Microwave Chicken? 144

Candied Herbs and Flowers 252

Canning: The Best Way to Express Your Love of Mason Jars 105

Caprese Salad Chicken 168

Cellaring—It's Where Root Vegetables Go to Chill 91

Chamomile Hair Brightener 249

Cheddar Deviled Eggs 228

Cherry Tomato Tomatillo Chutney 126

Chocolate Orange Torte 247

Cilantro Black Bean Dip 236

Classic Egg Nog 245

Classic Gingerbread 204

Common Ingredient Substitutes 145

Cream of Mushroom Soup 186

Creamy Chicken Bake 172

Cucumber and Green Bean Salad 183

DIY T-Shirt Bag 253

Dried Fruit Compote 218

Drunken Fruit Cobbler 117

Drunken Fruit Galettes 118

Drunken Fruit Whipped Pie 117

Drying—No Sunscreen Needed! 132

Dutch Oven Chicken Noodle Soup 163

Easy Artichoke Dip 238

Easy Cheesy Garlic Chicken 171

Easy Cheesy Soufflé 158

Easy Garden Gazpacho 185

Easy Hollandaise Sauce 151

Easy Sweet Potato Pie 224

Egg Custard 215

Egg-White Mask 248

Eggplant Dip 184

Eggshell Chalk 255

Essential Oils Air Freshener 254

Foraged Fried Eggs with Sage Butter 157

Freezer Chicken Stock 95

Freezer Eggs 96

Freezer Fruits 97

Freezer Poultry 93

Freezer Veggies 101

Freezing Peppers 104

Fresh Corn Fritter Patties 182

Fresh Garden Frittata 150

Fresh Guacamole Dip 233

Fresh Strawberry Mint Compote 219

Fried Zucchini Flowers 198

Garden Chicken Cacciatore 162

Garden Herb Cheese Balls 233

Garden Vegetable Dip 230

Garden-Fresh Bloody Mary 235

Grandma Jo's Orange Carrot Bread 202

Greek Style Green Beans 186

Greens and Beans 184

Guinness Beer Can Chicken 131

Herb Garden Radishes 190

Herbal Tea Companions 242

Herbed Sweet Potatoes 192

Honey Dijon Lime Chicken 172

Honey Lemon Rosemary Mask 248

Honey Sugar Shower Scrub 250

Honey Walnut Nougat 221

Hot Sorghum Cider 244

Italian Poached Eggs 152

Late-Summer Vegetable Soup 195

Mason Jar Method 80, 81

Mason Jar Party Favors and Gifts 257

Mediterranean Stuffed Tomatoes 193

Minted Grilled Zucchini 197

Minted Peas 189

Mulled Red Wine 243

My Mom's Apple Walnut Bundt Cake 214

Natural Food Coloring 256

Oatmeal Sprouts 81

Old Bay Vodka Corn Relish 124

Old Country French Onion Soup 187

Old-World Irish Mincemeat 109

Olive Potato Salad 190

Olive-Stuffed Chicken 169

Orange Tangerine Marmalade 114

Orchard Cabbage 181

Orchard Fruit Jelly 111

Pear Basil Preserves 110

Pesto Chicken 161

Pickled Onions 123

Pinto Bean Sprouts 80

Poor Man's Skillet Brandy Cake 213

Powdered Vegetable Soup Mix 137

Pure Vanilla Extract 115

Quick & Easy Applesauce 100

Quick & Easy Sandwich Pickles 122

Recipe Measurement Equivalency
    Cheat Sheet 147

Relaxing Herb Facial 249

Roasted Cauliflower 182

Rolled Oat Cakes with Blackberry
    Bourbon Sauce 206

Rosemary Lemon Granita 216

Rum Pot (Rumtopf) 120
Salt Curing and Smoking—The Ancient Art
    of Preservation 127
Salt Dough Ornaments 251
Sassy Sugar Snap Peas 189
Savory Scone Recipe 212
Savory Summer Squash 191
Scalloped Eggs 159
Scotch Chicken Eggs 151
Sea Salt Oatmeal Mask 249
Simple Syrup Recipe 100
Slow Cooker Chicken Goulash 173
Slow Cooker White Bean Chili 165
Spiced Milk 246
Spiced Red Cabbage 191
Spicy Chicken Quesadillas 167
Spring Egg Salad 154
Steam-Pressure Canning Method 108
Strawberry Daiquiri Jam 113
Strawberry Raspberry Kiwi Dip 240

Stuffed Acorn Squash 177
Stuffed Carrot Soup 181
Stuffed Mushrooms 232
Summer Skillet Stew 160
Sun-Speckled Pepper Eggs 155
Sunny Broccoli Salad 180
Sustainable Garden Chicken
    Meatballs 234
Sweet Scone Recipe 212
Tex-Mex Egg Burritos 154
Tomatillo Pie   194
Tomatillo Tart Salsa 112
Traditional Limoncello 119
Two-Minute Fruit Dip 239
Whole Honey-Glazed Chicken and
    Brown Bread Stuffing 166
Wild Blackberry Pie 223
Wine Biscuits 205
Winter Chicken Shepherd's Pie 170

About the Author

BARB WEBB is a sustainable living expert nesting in Appalachian Kentucky. When she's not chasing live chickens around the farm or engaging in mock Jedi battles, she's writing about country living and artisan culture.

Born under the earth sign Taurus, she arrived in the world ready to start nurturing, digging, and planting! She believes Irish cuisine is seriously under-valued and that if we simply open our minds and hearts to listen, the universe is an excellent guide.

Above all, she's incredibly thankful that her husband, three children, new grandchild, and all the chickens in the coop indulge her quirks, love of all things green, and desire to help others.

Connect with Barb and learn more about her work at SustainableChick.com.

TO OUR READERS

Viva Editions publishes books that inform, enlighten, and entertain. We do our best to bring you, the reader, quality books that celebrate life, inspire the mind, revive the spirit, and enhance lives all around. Our authors are practical visionaries: people who offer deep wisdom in a hopeful and helpful manner. Viva was launched with an attitude of growth and we want to spread our joy and offer our support and advice where we can to help you live the Viva way: vivaciously!

We're grateful for all our readers and want to keep bringing you books for inspired living. We invite you to write to us with your comments and suggestions, and what you'd like to see more of. You can also sign up for our online newsletter to learn about new titles, author events, and special offers.

Viva Editions
2246 Sixth St.
Berkeley, CA 94710
www.vivaeditions.com
(800) 780-2279
Follow us on Twitter @vivaeditions
Friend/fan us on Facebook